The
Collector's Encyclopedia
of
GAUDY DUTCH
and
WELSH

John A. Shuman III

The
Collector's Encyclopedia
of
GAUDY DUTCH
and
WELSH

COLLECTOR BOOKS

A Division of Schroeder Publishing Co., Inc.

The current values in this book should be used only as a guide. They are not intended to set prices, which vary from one section of the country to another. Auction prices as well as dealer prices vary greatly and are affected by condition as well as demand. Neither the Author nor the Publisher assumes responsibility for any losses that might be incurred as a result of consulting this guide.

DEDICATION

Gaudy Dutch Section

*In memory of
the late Reverend and Mrs. E. Richard Acker,
who had a deep fondness
and appreciation for Gaudy Dutch.*

Gaudy Welsh Section

*Dedicated to
Mr. John Hanebury, Jr.
and
Mrs. Suzanne Hanebury,
whose kindess and sharing
made this portion of the text possible.*

ACKNOWLEDGMENTS

GAUDY DUTCH

I am most appreciative to the following people and groups for their interest and cooperation: Mr. and Mrs. William Weiss; Mr. and Mrs. William Shutt; Mrs. Helen Cornog; Mr. and Mrs. Clyde Youtz; Dr. and Mrs. Richard W. Godshall; Mr. and Mrs. Horace Culbertson; Mr. Mark R. Stoudt; Annie S. Kemerer Museum; Berks County Historical Society; Franklin and Marshall College, Lancaster, PA; and the Historical Society of Montgomery County. Their assistance, courtesy, and sharing of time and valuable knowledge have helped make this portion of the book a reality.

❧

GAUDY WELSH

The following groups and individuals helped to make this portion of the text come alive with interesting facts and figures: The Philadelphia Free Library; Pottstown Public Library; Reading Public Library; Berks County Historical Library, Reading; Ursinus College, Collegeville; Kutztown University, Kutztown; Bloomsburg University, Bloomsburg; West Chester University, West Chester; West Chester Historical Society; Henry Ford Museum and Greenfield Village, Dearborn, Michigan; and Mr. John Hanebury, Jr. and his wife, Mrs. Suzanne Hanebury.

All of the Gaudy Dutch and Gaudy Welsh examples shown were personally handled, carefully inspected and photographed by the author.

TABLE OF CONTENTS
Gaudy Dutch

TABLE OF CONTENTS
Gaudy Welsh

TABLE OF CONTENTS
Gaudy Welsh

GAUDY DUTCH

*Includes a history of the people and their ware,
Gaudy Dutch patterns and their symbolism, and price guide.*

FOREWORD

Objectively, Part One of this book portrays in brilliant color 16 patterns of soft paste china collectively known as Gaudy Dutch. The term *earthenware* is now being used to describe the clay's consistency at lectures and symposiums. I hope to clarify the confusion among dealers and collectors involving the identification of any given pattern. Numerous typical shapes are illustrated and close-ups of the designs vividly depict the hand-decorated motifs. Identified impressed marks, and others, are listed as they appear on the pieces. Accurate descriptions, including heights and/or diameters, are given for each of the examples.

The introductory text includes a history of the various sects that moved to southeastern Pennsylvania in the late 17th century. Numerous events that prompted their emigrating from Germany and other countries are listed, plus the reasons they settled here.

The history of Gaudy Dutch is covered in its relationship to Japanese and Chinese Imari. These wares greatly influenced many English manufacturers.

Prices of over 30 rarities in Gaudy Dutch are given as determined by condition, shape, and pattern. Pennsylvania counties where Gaudy Dutch is most often seen, and a variety of community names originated by these people, are offered to the reader.

The basic principles of design (balance, rhythm, and dominance) that enable these English patterns to be successful artistically are discussed. One reference chart shows the meanings of numerous Gaudy Dutch motifs. A second helpful chart covers pattern variations in central themes, borders, underglazes, and overglazes.

A concise glossary, with over 50 terms, is included. This will assist the reader with the vocabulary on china. Useful ideas are suggested for acquiring Gaudy Dutch, taking care of it, and exhibiting it properly. Finally, biographical sources are noted for additional reading, and prices are volunteered for assorted shapes and patterns. My desire is that this section of the books will be enjoyable and helpful to you, serving as "a real Dutch treat!"

INTRODUCTION

Religious persecution (the Thirty Years' War, 1618-1648), the abolishment of the Edict of Nantes which forbade them to worship as they pleased, excessive taxation, French invasions that destroyed their farmland, combined with pestilence, hardships, and famine were all causes for Germans to depart from the Rhineland. Visiting Germany in 1671, and again in 1677, as a Quaker missionary, William Penn, advertised in letters and brochures seeking interested families to settle America. The leader of the ship *Concord*, Mennonite Francis Daniel Pastorius, had accepted an invitation from William Penn to inhabit vast areas of ground in southeastern Pennsylvania.

The trip was an arduous one. The lack of food and the long voyage crossing the Atlantic made the journey horrendous. Since shipping space was extremely limited, most left all worldly possessions behind and further agreed to become indentured servants. Some worked for two to seven years in servitude. Those that were physically strong and free-willed survived.

The main port of entry was Philadelphia. The ships *America* and *Concord* arrived in the new world in 1683; their inhabitants established a settlement on the outskirts of Philadelphia, known as Germantown. Others set out on their own exploring, settling, building, and decorating essential household items in order to live in their new environment. In the three months between April and July 1709, some 1,838 diversified and skilled workers arrived in Philadelphia. They comprised millers, bakers, butchers, tanners, saddlers, shoemakers, blacksmiths, tailors, hatters, stocking, cloth and linen weavers, engravers and silversmiths, brickmakers, masons, carpenters, coopers (barrel makers), turners (lathe workers), glassblowers and potters, lime burners, locksmiths, and barbers. In 1738, about 9,000 landed in Philadelphia. Their diversified skills and crafts were soon to be greatly recognized. Many also tilled the soil and cared for livestock. Inland waterways, rich limestone soil, and reports that no tithes were imposed caused great numbers to settle in southeastern Pennsylvania.

It would certainly be a misnomer, however, to think that all those who immigrated to this country from the 1680's to 1760's were of German descent. Factually, the term "Pennsylvania Dutch" or "Pennsylvania German" is rather inaccurate. It came from the Dutch peoples in New York who had been attracted by Queen Anne. The New Yorkers assigned this title to their fellow settlers who moved into the Delaware Valley of Pennsylvania. Actually, Penn's agents, when receiving these masses into the Philadelphia port, simply misrepresented them by calling all of them Palatines (Germans). Retaining their customs, language and religous faith stubbornly, a wide variety of conservative sects and nationalities encompassed: Moravians (Bethlehem), German Lutherans, Swiss Mennonites, Dunkards, Schwenkfelders, Amish from Flanders, French Huguenots, Swedes, Flemings, Dutch, Danes, Swabians, and Walloons. Since most of these people were Protestants, the church became both the language and religious center in their lives.

These past generations of hard working Americans were extremely imaginative in their uses and appreciation of art. Their tastes and talents, although primitive at times, reflected a very colorful chronicle of utilitarian items. Benjamin Franklin, in speaking of his contemporaries, stated, "Nothing is good or beautiful but in the measure that it is useful." An object, therefore, could not just exist for beauty's sake, but it also had to have a very special purpose in their everyday living. Their necessities then were given first priority. Later, their love for color was revealed in creations which they termed "just for fancy." The rich heritage of the Pennsylvania Dutch is revealed in their furniture, homespun linen, handmade quilts, colorful manuscripts, on their toleware, and through hex signs adorning their barns. Much stoneware and pottery was flourishing with birds, animals, flowers, and fruit. Some redware had decorative designs applied in slip; others had scratched designs, termed *sgraffito*.

Gaudy Dutch, a soft paste (earthenware) hand-decorated china, was an attempt by the English to imitate Chinese and Japanese wares known as Imari and Kakiemon. For the most part the ware can be classified as being opaque, although on rare occasion, some pieces examined reveal minimum translucency. In 1641, the Holland Dutch began importing great volumes of colorful Oriental ware into Europe. The ornamentations originated from designs found in woven and dyed fabrics. Underglaze colors were bluish black, and overglaze colors were predominately red. Gold was also used. Kakiemon porcelain was most often decorated with a blue underglaze, and by 1750, overglaze colors were similar to the Chinese. Kakiemon had a great influence on the European market through its characteristic shapes and decorations.

The first manufacturer of Gaudy Dutch in England was the Royal Worcester Pottery Works, located in Worcestershire. It was founded on June 4, 1751 by a deed of partnership, including 15 people. The most significant partner was Dr. John Wall. Several other English factories revived these wares during the 1800 era. According to some authorities, it did not appeal to the families in England with low incomes, thus an alternate market had to be found. After the War of 1812, it was sent to the American market. The ware was well received in Pennsylvania. It appears that English designers and decorators of this brilliantly colored china were familiar with customs, religious beliefs, and traditions, especially those of the Pennsylvania Dutch.

The term "Gaudy Dutch" originally came about since it referred to the Dutch importers who introduced gaudy Imari from Japan and China to Europe and England.

Names for the various patterns were perhaps coined in the 20th century by collectors and dealers for identification purposes. A Boston importer received great quantities of the ware in barrels and sold it for 12½¢ apiece. At one time Gaudy Dutch was plentiful and the cheapest available china of good quality.

The 16 patterns identified in the text have both similarities and differences. Mrs. Theresa Culbertson, a veteran dealer for many years, firmly believes that "No Name" is nothing more than a variant of the "Single Rose" pattern. Mr. Clyde Youtz, another Pennsylvania dealer for numerous years, never recalls having a piece of "No Name." Perhaps because it might be a variant helps to explain why sets have not been found, thus, its extreme rarity. Maybe the collector should seek examples of only 15 patterns! The techniques and motifs illustrate three major aspects: large and small areas shaded in yellows and greens, large areas in shades of red overglaze, and large areas in blue underglaze. In some patterns, the blue is decorated with an overglaze; in others it is not. A variety of borders exists in the patterns, which may be called single and double borders. Some transitional examples, or hybrids, in one of the 16 patterns have luster applied to them. This variant type technically should not be categorized or purchased as Gaudy Dutch. Pieces are occasionally found impressed "WOOD" or "RILEY." Still rarer impressed marks are "DAVENPORT" or "ROGERS." None of the dealers or collectors to whom I have spoken ever recalled seeing any names impressed in shapes other than assorted plate sizes. If you own an example other than a plate impressed with one of these names, it would be considered extremely rare. A reproduction of this ware, impressed "CYBIS," was made in Trenton, New Jersey from 1949 to 1950. Authentic cups and saucers may be found with sides that are round, straight, or having a median ridge. Hollow pieces are either oblong or round, and plates may be ridged or flat on the underside.

From an artistic viewpoint, all of the patterns successfully conform to three basic principles of design, namely balance, rhythm, and dominance. In my discussion I will limit myself to examples of flatware, enabling the reader to visualize more readily these concepts.

Asymmetrically, the "Leaf" and the "Oyster" patterns serve as our examples. The greater part of the large leaf falls to the left, joined by one and a half small pink flowers and a blue leaf. Smaller portions of the large leaf are on the right, accompanied by two and a half pink flowers and a blue leaf. The left side of the "Oyster" pattern shows a large flower with a portion of the oyster superimposed and a leaf on the ground below. The right side displays a thistle, a small flower, the rest of the oyster superimposed, plus a leaf and a small round object on the ground (perhaps a pearl). Symmetrically, I will discuss the centrally located "Butterfly." The left portion of the butterfly includes a branch with blue fruit and a flower. Below the butterfly is a spray of leaves and a blue semicircle, highlighted with leaves and grass. The right side is identical, except a small vase rests on the semicircle with a flower emanating from it.

The "Dahlia" pattern is a good example of rhythm, with its long curving strokes uninhibited by a narrow blue border. The central flower is red overglaze. This color is also incorporated in the bud and open flower on the left and carried through in the buds on the right. The large leaves in "Dahlia," not including the blue triple leaf trimmed in yellow, are half yellow and green. The small leaves are either entirely green or green over blue. The border is blue, edged in reddish brown.

To illustrate dominance, the "War Bonnet" is an excellent choice. The eye is drawn to the concentration of dark blue in the center of the pattern. The bonnet and the four feathers, along with the leaf and bud above, are outlined in yellow. The large shaded red peony may be found in assorted shapes and sizes on various examples. Its color is complimented by four smaller flowers which do not always appear in the same positions.

It must be understood, however, in the discussions on balance, rhythm, and dominance that I have made general, rather than specific, statements. This is understandable, since all pieces of this ware were decorated freely by hand. Thus, no two artists working in the same, or different, factory would be able to place each motif in exactly the same spot over and over.

I have included a price guide on Gaudy Dutch, although prices have escalated to a point where those that own and collect this china know its value. Thus, bargains in this ware are practically nonexistent, and those desirous of acquiring it will pay the going market rate at that time. Keep in mind that most antiques appreciate annually from 10 to 15%. For the most part, Gaudy Dutch pricing is determined by the following factors: condition, pattern, and shape. Generally, prices have inflated until an article today can be worth a thousand times or more its original cost. The value of this ware, and its desirability, is truly one of the anachronisms in the world of collecting. We must remember that the law of supply and demand takes precedence in this case. It is, perhaps, one of the soundest investments today in china for those who enjoy this particular type of colorful artistry.

An outstanding collection of Gaudy Dutch was sold at the Pennypacker Auction Centre, 1540 New Holland Road, Kenhorst (Reading), Pennsylvania on October 19, 1970. This was the famous Wharton Sinkler Collection (Chestnut Hill, Pennsylvania) and consisted of over 155 select pieces, many of them rarities. Examples at the sale and the prices they commanded were:

1. Extremely rare center Butterfly coffee pot - $6,400.00.
2. Rare central Butterfly 10" plate, mint - $800.00.
3. Three-piece Carnation creamer, sugar and teapot - $1,500.00.
4. Extremely rare Double Rose 17" platter - $3,100.00.
5. Rare Double Rose sugar bowl, eagle handles, mint - $900.00.
6. Strawflower plate, 8¼", marked "RILEY," mint - $475.00.
7. Rare Strawflower toddy plate, 5½", marked "RILEY," mint - $775.00.
8. Rare Dahlia teapot, body checks - $600.00.
9. Rare Sunflower waste bowl, 6¼" diameter - $300.00.
10. Sunflower plate, 10", mint - $625.00.
11. Rare orange Oyster helmet-shaped teapot, imperfect - $500.00.
12. Yellow Oyster plate, 10", leaf flake - $400.00.
13. War Bonnet cup and saucer, mint - $350.00.
14. Extremely rare War Bonnet pitcher, 6" - $850.00.
15. Extremely rare War Bonnet helmet-shaped coffee pot, one of only two known to exist - $4,000.00.
16. Dove plate, blue band, 9¼", mint - $375.00.
17. Dove creamer, mint - $400.00.
18. Dove cup and saucer, imperfect - $130.00.
19. Rare "RILEY" Zinnia plate, 8⅜", mint - $475.00.
20. Rare "RILEY" Primrose plate, 8½" - $475.00.
21. Rare Urn teapot, spider mark on the body - $575.00.
22. Urn plate, 8⅛", mint - $240.00.
23. Single Rose round sugar bowl, shell handles, beehive finial, discolored - $375.00.
24. Single Rose soup dish, 10", mint - $375.00.
25. Single Rose plate, 5⅝", chip on the reverse - $110.00.
26. Unusual Single Rose plate, 9¾", mint - $350.00.
27. Rare Grape cup plate, 3⅜" - $300.00.
28. Grape teapot, spider mark on the body - $325.00.
29. Rare Grape teapot, repair on the spout - $400.00.
30. Grape porridge plate, 7⅛", cracked - $50.00.

In addition to these items and others sold at Pennypacker's Centre over the years, one other rarity in Gaudy Dutch is worth mentioning. This example, from the Walter K. Durham Collection, a Philadelphia architect, was sold on October 14, 1974. The small rectangular two-piece box in Gaudy Dutch was in the "Single Rose" pattern and described as a quill box, or brush holder. It sold for $2,600.00!

Some of the Gaudy Dutch items from the Whaton Sinkler Collection sold at the Pennypacker Auction Centre October 19, 1970.

Close-up of central Butterfly variant.

Central Butterfly, unusual detail, impressed "H" on the bottom. Saucer - 5¼" in diameter.

Central Butterfly cup - 2¼" high, 3⅝" in diameter; saucer - 5½" in diameter. Examples are especially fine due to detail in flowers. *Horace Culbertson*.

Butterfly waste bowl - 5⅛" across, 2⅞" high.

Butterfly and Water Lily plate, variant, impressed six-sided rosette - 7¼" in diameter.

CARNATION

Carnation close-up.

Carnation pattern - cup, 2½" high; saucer, 5½" in diameter; plate, 7⅜" in diameter.
Berks County Historical Society.

Carnation soup bowl - 8¼" diameter.

DAHLIA

Close-up of Dahlia pattern.

Dahlia cup, 2¼" high, 3⅝" diameter; saucer 5⁷⁄₁₆" diameter. *Horace Culbertson.*

Beautiful Dahlia teapot, oblong finial on lid, 6" to the top.

DOUBLE ROSE

Double Rose close-up.

Double Rose soup plate, 9⅝".

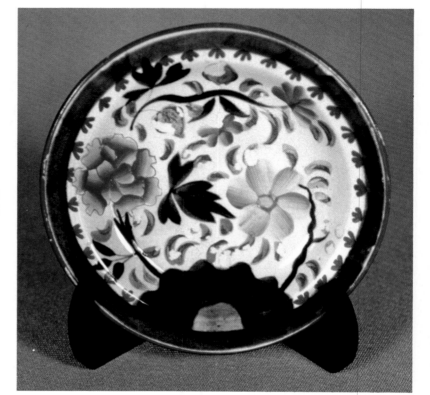

Double Rose toddy plate, 3½" in diameter. Notice there is only one mound, impressed " $\frac{5}{23}$ " on the back. *Berks County Historical Society*.

Double Rose teapot, flower finial, scalloped gallery top, 6½" high, impressed on the base "12," eight-sided rosette on the bottom.

Double Rose cup - 2³/₁₆" high, 3½" diameter; saucer - 5½" diameter. Cobalt blue "5" underglazed on both pieces. Two green lines on cup. *Horace Culbertson.*

Double Rose sugar bowl, scalloped gallery top, flower finial, 5½" high.
Historial Society of Montgomery County.

Side view of Double Rose sugar bowl, note the handle.

DOVE

Close-up of Dove.

Dove pattern cup - 2½" high; saucer - 5½" in diameter.

Dove cup and saucer with unusual scalloped edges, salmon rims. Cup - 3½" diameter, 2¼" high. Saucer - 5⅜" diameter. *Horace Culbertson.*

Dove creamer, 4⅜" to top of handle.

Dove sugar bowl, 5⅜" high to top of finial.

Side view of Dove sugar bowl showing shell handle.

GRAPE

Grape close-up.

Comparison of two Grape plates. Notice difference in ground, borders, flowers, and shading. Left - 8¼" diameter; right - 7" diameter. Both have "$\frac{2}{1036}$" in red on the backs.

Comparison of two cups and saucers in the Grape pattern. Note shapes of cups, shading on grapes, and ground contours. Both cups are 2¼" high. Both saucers are 5⅝" in diameter.

Grape handled cup and saucer, later examples. Saucer - 5½" diameter. Cup - 3½" diameter, 2⁵⁄₁₆" high. *Horace Culbertson.*

Grape teapot, 6¼" to top of finial. Numbered "$\frac{2}{1036}$" in red on the base.

Grape teapot, scalloped gallery rim, floral finial, 6½" high, impressed eight-sided rosette and a cobalt "X" on the bottom. *Historical Society of Montgomery County.*

LEAF

Leaf close-up.

Leaf pattern creamer, 5½" to top of handle. Sugar bowl - 5¾" to top of flower finial, coffin handles.

Teapot in Leaf pattern, 7¼" to top of finial, repaired handle, "8" impressed on the bottom.

Leaf cup and saucer. Saucer has impressed "11," also within a circle "E WOOD & SONS BURSLEM SEMICHINA WARRANTED," plus an eagle and shield. Cup - 3¼" diameter, 2½" high. Saucer - 5¾" diameter. *Horace Culbertson.*

NO NAME

No Name close-up.

No Name cup and saucer, dark blue border, yellow edges. Cup - 2¼" high, 3½" diameter. Saucer - 5¼" diameter. *Horace Culbertson.*

OYSTER

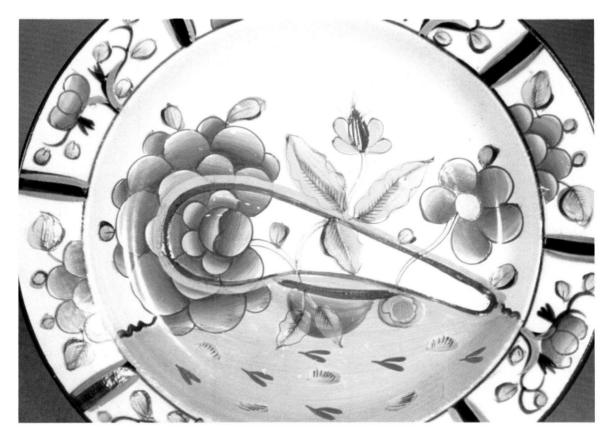

Close-up of Oyster pattern.

Oyster creamer - 4⅜" high to top of handle. Plate - 7⁵⁄₁₆" in diameter, "10" impressed on the back. *Berks County Historical Society.*

Oyster saucer with yellow ground, 5⅜" diameter.

Oyster waste bowl, 5⅜" diameter, height 2¹¹⁄₁₆".

Close-up of King's Rose Oyster variant.

King's Rose Oyster soup plate, 10" in diameter, impressed "8" on the bottom.

PRIMROSE

Primrose close-up.

Primrose plate, 8¼" in diameter, impressed "RILEY" on the underside.

Primrose cup and saucer. Note unusual shape of cup. Cup - 2½" high, 3⅝" diameter; saucer - 5½" diameter. *Horace Culbertson.*

Primrose toddy, impressed nine-sided rosette, 4½" in diameter.

SINGLE ROSE

Close-up of Single Rose.

Single Rose plate, 8⅛" in diameter.

Comparison of two Single Rose cups and saucers. Technically, the right hand example should not be classified as Gaudy Dutch because of the pink luster edge. Also, this example has no fence, and the flowers and leaves are shaped and shaded differently. Left: cup - 2⅜" high; saucer - 5½" in diameter. Right: cup - 2¼" high; saucer - 5⅝" in diameter. *Berks County Historical Society.*

Single Rose creamer, 4¾" to top of handle.

Single Rose waste bowl, 6⁵⁄₁₆" diameter, 2¹⁵⁄₁₆" height. *Berks County Historical Society*.

STRAWFLOWER

Strawflower close-up.

Mint Strawflower soup plate, 8¼" diameter, impressed "RILEY" on back. *Berks County Historical Society.*

Strawflower pattern plate, 10" diameter, impressed "RILEY." *Horace Culbertson.*

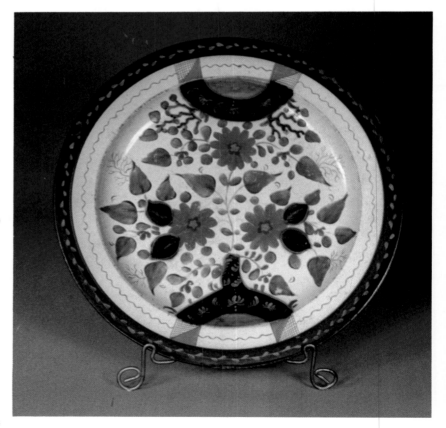

SUNFLOWER

Sunflower close-up.

Sunflower plate, 9¾" across. "D" impressed on the reverse side.

Sunflower cup - 2⅜" high; saucer - 5½" diameter.

Sunflower waste bowl - 3³⁄₁₆" high, 6½" diameter. *Clyde Youtz*.

URN

Close-up of Urn.

Urn plate, 9¾" in diameter.

Urn plate, 7⅜" in diameter, slight border variation.

Urn cup - 2½" high; saucer - 5½" diameter. Urn plate - 8¼" diameter, impressed "11" on the reverse. *Berks County Historical Society*.

Urn waste bowl, slight discoloration, height 3", diameter 6¼". *Annie S. Kemerer Museum.*

Urn sugar bowl, 5½" to top of finial. Same shell handles as Dove sugar bowl.

Urn teapot, 6½" to top of finial.

WAR BONNET

War Bonnet close-up.

War Bonnet plate, 7⅛" diameter. Pattern number " $\frac{2}{1037}$ " in red on the back.

War Bonnet cup plate, diameter 4", " $\frac{2}{1037}$ " on the back. Note the different artistic rendition in comparison to the plate above. *Clyde Youtz.*

War Bonnet cup - 2½" high; saucer - 5½" diameter. Cup has two short red brush strokes on the underside; saucer has three short green brush strokes on the back.

War Bonnet creamer, 4½" to top of handle, "$\frac{2}{1037}$" on the base in red.

Reverse of War Bonnet Creamer.

ZINNIA

Close-up of Zinnia pattern.

Zinnia plate, diameter 8¼". "RILEY" impressed on the underside.

Close-up of impressed "RILEY" mark.

Close-up of Wood impression.

Shown is a colored flyer issued some years ago by the Henry Ford Museum and Greenfield Village featuring their adaptation of the Butterfly pattern in Gaudy Dutch. Made in Ironstone china by Miles Mason, famed the world over for their durability, the collection consisted of dinnerware and accessories.

The reverse of the flyer shows 12 introductory selections, not to scale that were available. They included a 10½" dinner plate, 8" salad plate, 6" wide bread and butter plate, 5½" teapot, tea/coffee cup and saucer, 9" coffee pot, 9¾" serving bowl, sugar bowl with lid, 2⅞" creamer, 6½" cereal bowl, 3½" marmalade jar with lid and saucer, and a 5" high candy jar with lid. Widths are given for the dinner plate, salad plate, bread and butter plate, serving bowl and cereal bowl. All other measurements given are heights. The retail prices for these discontinued items each were: dinner plate, $18.50; salad plate, $15.50; bread/butter plate, $12.50; cereal bowl, $15.50; cup and saucer, $18.50 a set; tea cup and saucer, $18.50 a set; covered sugar bowl, $27.50; creamer, $15.00; coffee pot, $57.50; teapot, $65.00; covered marmalade jar with saucer, $22.50 a set; covered candy jar, $29.50; serving bowl, $35.00; place setting, $65.00 a set; bud vase, $19.50; oblong sweets dish, $17.50; coaster, $8.00; nut bowl, $22.50 and a temple jar with lid, $25.00 a set.

SYMBOLISM IN GAUDY DUTCH

PATTERNS

1.	Butterfly	B.
2.	Carnation	C.
3.	Dahlia	D.
4.	Double Rose	D.R.
5.	Dove	Do.
6.	Grape	G.
7.	Leaf	L.
8.	No Name	N.N.
9.	Oyster	O.
10.	Primrose	P.
11.	Single Rose	S.R.
12.	Strawflower	St.
13.	Sunflower	Su.
14.	Urn	U.
15.	War Bonnet	W.B.
16.	Zinnia	Z.

SYMBOLS DEFINED

1.	Dove	(Bliss)
2.	Urn	(Water of Life)
3.	Tree of Life	(Phases of each generation)
4.	Sun Spirals/Arc of summer, winter solstice	(Seasons)
5.	The Holy Trinity	(Father, Son, Holy Ghost)
6.	Tables of the Decalogue	(Ten Commandments)
7.	Heart	(All-bearing Mother Earth)
8.	Drooping Branches, Fallen Leaves, Flowers in Various Phases	(Life's Stages)

SYMBOLS

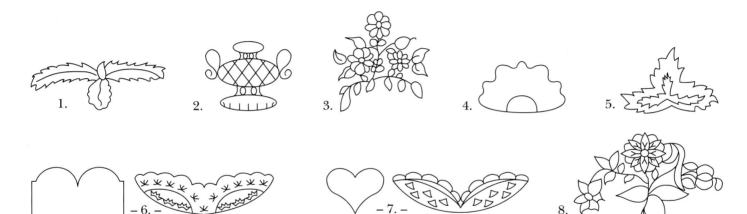

This chart illustrates symbols common to the "Dutch" heritage. Coordinate the symbols (1-8) with the pattern abbreviations (1-16). Key the pattern abbreviations found in various blocks to the artistic symbols. Example: In pattern number 1 (Butterfly) the "B." appears opposite symbols 2, 3, 6 and 7. Thus, the Butterfly pattern includes Urn, Tree of Life, Table of the Decalogue and the Heart.

PATTERNS

SYMBOLS	1	2	3	4	5	6	7	8	9	10	11	12	13	14	15	16
1					Do.											
2	B.											St.		U.		Z.
3	B.	C.	D.		Do.	G.	L.	N.N.		P.	S.R.	St.	Su.	U.	W.B.	Z.
4				D.R.		G.		N.N.	O.		S.R.	St.				
5		C.	D.	D.R.	Do.	G.	L.	N.N.	O.	P.	S.R.	St.	Su.	U.		Z.
6	B.	C.								P.						
7	B.	C.								P.						
8		C.	D.	D.R.	Do.	G.		N.N.	O.	P.		St.	Su.	U.	W.B.	Z.

AVAILABILITY OF PATTERNS

1. Butterfly ....Obtainable
2. Carnation ....Obtainable
3. Dahlia ....Rare
4. Double Rose ....Obtainable
5. Dove ....Most Common
6. Grape ....Rare
7. Leaf..Rare
8. No Name ....Extremely Rare
9. Oyster ....Most Common
10. Primrose ....Rare
11. Single Rose ....Most Common
12. Strawflower ....Rare
13. Sunflower ....Obtainable
14. Urn ....Most Common
15. War Bonnet ....Most Common
16. Zinnia ....Rare

SOME PATTERN VARIATIONS IN GAUDY DUTCH

Pattern	Red edge	Green or Yellow edge	Blue underglaze border/ yellow overglaze	Panel border/ division in blue underglaze trimmed in yellow	Wavy red line border	Four squares connected to the border	Single border
Butterfly	✓		✓		✓		✓
Carnation	✓		✓		✓ Also with Leaves		✓
Dahlia	✓		✓ No Yellow Overglaze				✓
Double Rose	✓		✓ No Yellow Overglaze				✓
Dove	✓		✓ No Yellow Overglaze/ Covered with red				✓
Grape	✓		✓		✓		✓
Leaf	✓		✓				✓
No Name		✓					✓
Oyster	✓			✓			✓
Primrose	✓		✓		✓		✓
Single Rose	✓		✓		✓ Also with Leaves		✓
Strawflower	✓		✓		✓	✓ Variant	
Sunflower	✓		✓		✓ Also with Leaves		✓
Urn	✓			✓			✓
War Bonnet	✓			✓			✓
Zinnia	✓		✓				

SOME PATTERN VARIATIONS IN GAUDY DUTCH

Pattern	Double Border	Red separates border from central design	Yellow line separates green central design	Rectangular fence	Triple Leaf	All parts outlined in blue underglaze	Patterns on cups and bowls are reversed
Butterfly	✔	✔			✔		
Carnation	✔	✔			✔		
Dahlia	✔	✔		✔	✔ Smooth		
Double Rose		✔			✔		
Dove		✔			✔		✔
Grape					✔		
Leaf			✔		✔		
No Name			✔	✔ Like S. Rose Except Shading	✔	✔	
Oyster					✔ Smooth		
Primrose	✔	✔		✔	✔		
Single Rose	✔	✔			✔		
Strawflower	✔						
Sunflower	✔	✔			✔ Smooth		✔
Urn	✔				✔		
War Bonnet							
Zinnia	✔	✔			✔		

GLOSSARY

Amish: An orthodox Anabaptist sect that separated from the Mennonites in the late 17th century. Today they live primarily in southeastern Pennsylvania. Their religion is simple and like that of early Christians. Although they are strict in their dress, they love color used in other ways. One of their best loved colors is blue, hence the name Amish blue. It is combined with white to yield Prussian blue, navy blue, cobalt and other hues.

Asymmetrical balance: A design arranged so that one half is different from the other. Example: a large object on one side balancing two or three small objects on the other side.

Biscuit: Porcelain, stoneware or pottery after a low preliminary firing, before the glaze firing.

Ceramics: General term for all types of pottery and porcelain.

Chip: A small flake missing usually from an edge as a result of just use and/or misuse.

Cuplin': A corrupted word form for handleless cups, older than those with handles.

"CYBIS": An impressed signature on reproduced hard opaque porcelain. Examples are shaped differently than antiques, and the hard glaze is quite shiny.

"DAVENPORT": A variety of impressed marks usually incorporating the family name and an anchor. Some marks will also include a crown and the words "LONGPORT" and "STAFFORDSHIRE"; a later impressed mark was "D." Established by John Davenport in 1794, inherited by his sons, William and Henry, in 1848, and prospered until 1887.

Design: A well-planned arrangement.

Discoloration: Imbedded brownish stain which detracts from the beauty and the value of the piece. Careful cleaning sometimes will remove this. There is always the risk of destroying the colors in the overglaze.

Dominance: When one part of an art work is stronger or more important than any other part. Examples: a larger shape, a color used more often than others, or a brighter color.

Dunkards: A German-American Baptist sect opposed to military service and taking office. They baptized their young by triple immersion.

Flourished: Freehand artistry similar to that used in ornate penmanship.

Gaudyware: A name given collectively to gay English earthenware with brilliantly colored floral patterns. At one time it was believed that these wares were made in Pennsylvania by the "Dutch." The term includes Gaudy Dutch, Gaudy Welsh and Gaudy Ironstone.

Gaudy Dutch: A term referring to the sixteen brilliantly colored patterns in this lightweight soft paste ware. Most frequently found in Pennsylvania, but occasionally in other states too. Made about 1790 to 1825.

Gaudy Welsh: A translucent porcelain made after 1820, usually possessing a resonance (flat pieces) when tapped. It was made in full table service with blue as an underglaze and other vibrant colors used as overglazes. The early ware is of a higher quality, with later export examples bearing the manufacturer's name. They are both thicker and heavier by weight. Patterns include: Tulip, Oyster, Morning Glory, Grape, Urn, Wagon Wheel, Shanghai, Daisy and Chain, and Strawberry.

Gaudy Ironstone: A china manufactured in the early 1850's decorated in the Imari style. It is thick and heavy and often has an impressed mark. The blue underglaze characteristically bleeds through to the other side of the example. Bright colors and luster were incorporated in the designs. Some patterns by name are: Seeing Eye, Blackberry, Carnation, Urn, Butterfly, Strawberry, Pinwheel, Morning Glory, and Grape. "WALLEY," "WALKER," "IRONSTONE," "PARIS WHITE IRONSTONE CHINA," "TAVOY," "WASHINGTON," "NIAGARA SHAPE," and "PEARL WHITE" are a few of the impressed marks found. This ware was not extremely popular and, after just a few years, was taken off the market.

Glaze: Shiny, glass-like substance, waterproofing, strengthening and enhancing the colors of the piece. Gaudy Dutch has a transparent glaze fired to its surface.

Greenware: Unfinished clay which is air dried to remove moisture before it can be safely fired.

Hair line: See spider mark.

Handled Cup: First made during the last quarter of the 18th century. This innovation toward polite etiquette permitted the saucer or bowl to be somewhat flattened, similar to the proportions of today.

Hard paste: A true porcelain requiring 1450 degrees Celsius to fuse properly. Varied ingredients include kaolin (white clay), ground glass, soapstone, and bone ash. Whereas the Chinese stored their unfired clay for decades before use, the English considered eight months a sufficient waiting period.

Hollow ware: Vessels or containers, such as teapots, pitchers, bowls, coffee pots, creamers, cups and saucers.

Huguenots: French Protestants of the 16th and 17th centuries.

Impressed mark: Stamp or imprint on the underside of a piece, identifying its maker, accomplished before firing.

"Just for fancy": Used decoratively but not functionally, a term coined in the Dutch country.

Kiln: An oven for baking or firing ceramics.

Luster: A metallic sheen used on pottery. Oxides of gold and silver were used.

Median: Centrally located.

Mennonite: Member of a true Christian sect, founded in the 16th century by Menno Simons, a former Catholic priest. Those opposed to military service, holding public office, or taking oaths.

Mint: Fresh, original condition.

Molding: Wet clay, or slip, was poured into plaster of Paris molds. The clay dried quickly; much moisture was absorbed by the plaster. The shaped piece was easily removed, cleaned, and prepared for firing.

Moravians: A Protestant denomination founded in 1722 in Saxony by Hussite emigrants from Moravia, Czechoslovakia.

Opaque: Not penetrable by light.

Overglaze: Orange, yellow, red, pink, green, and rust hues applied on top of the glaze and refired.

Patterns: Gaudy Dutch consists of 16 artistic and decoratively colored designs.

Polychrome: Brilliant coloration used by the Pennsylvania Dutch on their furniture, barns, toleware, in their quilts, and on their manuscripts. Included because of the similarities between the colors on Gaudy Dutch and those used in their everyday lives.

Rare: Uncommon, unusual, highly valued.

Redware: Characteristic clay found in Pennsylvania, having a terra cotta hue when fired.

Repaired: Skillfully mended, painted, and glazed. Formulas for this type of work are closely guarded secrets. Examples: finial on a lid, spout on a teapot, etc.

Rhythm: Colors, lines, shapes, and textures are similar to others in the art work. Examples: long curving lines, repetition of color.

"RILEY": Impressed mark. Found on some examples of Zinnia, Strawflower, Primrose, and Single Rose.

Riley, John and Richard: 1802-1826.

Rileyware: Referred to Gaudy Dutch in the early years, as Riley was one of the potters who made it and impressed his name on the pieces before they were fired.

"ROGERS": Impressed Longport mark seldom found, John Rogers and Son. About 1800-1835.

Roseware: Various patterns and their variants including King's Rose, Queen's Rose, Adams Rose, Cabbage Rose, and a combined Strawberry and Rose.

Schwenkfelder: Founded by the exiled Silesian nobleman, Caspar Schwenckfeld von Ossig (1489-1561), who advocated fellowship and liberty of religious belief. A writer, preacher, scholar, and reformer, his following of 180 departed for America in 1734. They spent a brief time in Holland, where Mennonite merchants in Haarlem financed their ship passage to Pennsylvania and donated 224 Rix Dollars to fund the poor on arrival. This jesture freed the Schwenkfelders from the slavery of the "redemptioner." The group landed in Philadelphia on September 22, 1734. The Society of Schwenkfelders was officially formed in 1782. The present day sect consists of Schwenkfelder Churches in Lansdale, Philadelphia, Palm, Norristown, and Worcester, Pennsylvania, with a membership totaling about 2,500.

Script pattern number: Number on the reverse side of some pieces, referring to their pattern number.

Sgraffito: Decoration on pottery done by scratching through one surface, revealing a second contrasting color underneath.

Slip: A creamy consistency of clay and water, usually white or yellow. Used as a decorative device.

Soft paste: A mixture of substances consisting of sand, clay, and glass used to create an artificial porcelain. It is sometimes translucent, less brittle than hard paste, and the body and glaze blend easily during firing. Only about 1100 degrees Celsius were needed to fuse enamels and glazes to the bodies. Also sensitive to sudden temperature changes.

Spider mark: Flaw consisting of a crack in the glaze or a thin line fracture.

Stilt mark: Minute triangular three prong marks on the reverse side of an example, where the piece was supported in the kiln while being fired.

Strawberry: A type of soft paste made in the 1800's in assorted tablewares. Many variants in design, including luster, can be found. The raised Strawberry design is especially unusual and beautiful.

Swabians: Inhabitants in the southwestern regions of Germany.

Symmetrical balance: Most of the objects are placed in the center, or one half of a work of art looks similar to the other.

Translucent: Capable of transmitting light; soft paste has a very minimum of translucency in areas where the clay is thin.

Underglaze: Blue decoration applied while the piece is in its biscuit state. This coloration is often referred to as cobalt blue.

Variations: Individual differences created by artists in numerous factories while decorating the borders and central designs. Some rare variant examples may have a transfer border.

Walloons: French peoples living in southern and southeastern Belgium and adjoining regions of France.

Wood, Enoch and Sons, Burslem: From 1819.

"WOOD": Impressed mark seldom seen on Gaudy Dutch. When found it will occur on the Grape and Single Rose patterns. Also seen on the Leaf pattern; perhaps it may occur on others.

A potter applying handles. *The Penny Magazine*, **February 1843.**
(See Glossary - "Handled Cup.")

ACQUISITION, CARE, AND EXHIBITION

Acquisition

Some collectors of Gaudy Dutch are fortunate enough to get their start through an inheritance. Others, who appreciate the beauty and the rarity of this early earthenware, may be able to secure it privately through a collector. Quality antique shops and large primitive antique shows would be two excellent sources for purchases. It always pays to conduct business with a reputable dealer and one who will stand behind his merchandise in writing. Large choice collections often come on the market through various highly advertised catalogue auctions. In this case it is wise to acquire a booklet and inspect the merchandise critically before it is sold. Antique publications, on occasion, will offer assorted shapes and patterns in Gaudy Dutch for sale. Because of the fragile character of the ware, buying pieces through the mail should be an alternate to transporting it personally. It is very infrequent that pieces would be found in thrift shops, at flea markets or house auctions.

Care

This china should be washed occasionally with a soft cloth and a very mild soap. Damp and soft dry cloths might be sufficient. On no occasion should the pieces be left on a drain board to dry. Harsh soaps and abrasives are absolutely taboo. Although changes in temperature are not as critical with china as they are in glass, items should never be placed in an oven, dishwasher, or refrigerator. It certainly would seem impractical, after investing in this soft paste, to use it as tableware. Damage could easily result to the surface from using a sharp knife. Broken examples may be repaired by a professional if the owner feels it is worthwhile and not too costly. Also, colors may be restored to their original state if they are badly flaked. Some people frown on this procedure and try to procure examples in mint condition; these, of course, command a higher selling price.

Storage can be very valuable, but done incorrectly, can be detrimental. All objects should be cleaned and then carefully wrapped in soft white tissue paper. An extra padding of newspaper may be wrapped over the outside. The paper may be secured with tape, but keep in mind that tape will readily dry out. Newspapers should not be placed next to the objects, as the print could come off on the surface designs. Other assorted packing materials may be used to cushion the pieces. Small sturdy boxes with a flap should be employed to keep away dust and dirt. Do not stack a number of pieces upon one another to create an undue weight. The containers should be carefully sealed and labeled, stored where they will not be bumped or kicked, and in a fairly constant temperature away from dampness.

Exhibition

Assorted cupboards with grooves or rails provide an excellent way of showing platters, plates, and saucers. Hollow ware, set on the same shelves, will complement these examples. Collectors often choose to use contemporary glass cases with indirect lighting to enhance their acquisitions. A clever interior decorator could easily incorporate the vivid Dutch colors to accentuate the decor of a room. Metal stands, covered with soft rubber, or wooden holders may be used to secure pieces. It would not be advisable to display plates in metal holders on walls, as vibrations or a poorly secured nail could result in a terrible loss for the owner.

BIBLIOGRAPHY

Aldridge, Eileen. *Porcelain.* New York: Bantam Books, 1971.

Barba, Dr. Preston A. "Folk Art On Pennsylvania German Tombstones," *The Historical Review of Berks County,* (January-March 1955), Volume XX, Number 2.

Bronner, Edwin B. *William Penn's "Holy Experiment" 1681-1701.* Philadelphia: Temple University Press, 1962.

Coffin, Margaret Mattison. "Dictionary of American Painted Furniture," *Woman's Day,* (July 1966), 25-32.

Cole, Ann Kilborn. *Antiques.* New York: Collier Books, 1965.

Cole, Ann Kilborn. *The Golden Guide to American Antiques.* New York: Golden Press, 1967.

Comstock, Helen (ed.) *The Concise Encyclopedia of American Antiques.* New York: Hawthorn Books, Incorporated, 1969.

Davidson, Marshall B. (ed.) *The American Heritage History of Colonial Antiques.* New York: American Heritage Publishing Company, Incorporated, 1967.

Day, Sherman. *Historical Collection of the State of Pennsylvania.* New York: Ira J. Friedman, Incorporated, 1969.

Drepperd, Carl W. *A Dictionary of American Antiques.* New York: Award Books, 1968.

Fox, Eleanor J. and Edward G. *Gaudy Dutch.* Pottsville, Pennsylvania: Pamphlet privately printed, 1968.

Henshaw, Keith, and Donald Cowie. *Antique Collector's Dictionary.* New York: Gramercy Publishing Company, 1962.

Hubbard, Guy, and Mary J. Rouse. *Art 5 - Meaning, Method, and Media.* Westchester, Illinois: Benefic Press, 1972.

Hughes, G. Bernard. *The Collector's Pocket Book of China.* New York: Award Books, 1970.

Kovel, Ralph and Terry. *Know Your Antiques.* New York: Crown Publishers, Incorporated, 1967.

Laidacker, Sam. *The American Antiques Collector.* Summer 1943, Volume III, Number 2. Bloomsburg, Pennsylvania: Privately printed, 1943.

Laidacker, Sam. *The American Antiques Collector.* Spring 1949, Volume III, Number 7. Bristol, Pennsylvania: Privately printed, 1949.

Laidacker, Sam. *The American Antiques Collector.* Volume III, Number 8. Bristol, Pennsylvania: Privately printed, 1952.

Laidacker, Sam. *Anglo-American China Part I.* Bristol, Pennsylvania: Privately printed, 1954.

Laidacker, Sam. *Auction Supplement to The Standard Catalogue of Anglo-American China.* May 1938 to June 1944. Scranton, Pennsylvania: Privately printed, 1944.

Laidacker, Sam. *Auction Supplement to The Standard Catalogue of Anglo-American China.* June 1944 to January 1949. Bristol, Pennsylvania: Privately printed, 1949.

Pennypacker *Americana Antique Auction.* October 14, 1974. Volume XVIII, Number 9. Kenhorst, Pennsylvania: Privately printed, 1974.

Pennypacker *Gaudy Dutch China Collection.* October 19, 1970. Volume 14, Number 14. Kenhorst, Pennsylvania: Privately printed, 1970.

Robacker, Earl F. *Touch of the Dutchland.* New York: A.S. Barnes and Company, Incorporated, 1965.

Soderlund, Jean R. (ed.) *William Penn and the founding of Pennsylvania 1680-1684.* Philadelphia: University of Pennsylvania Press, 1983.

Wallower, Lucille. *Colonial Pennsylvania.* New York: Thomas Nelson and Sons, 1969.

ADDITIONAL READING

Borneman, Henry S. *Pennsylvania German Bookplates.* Philadelphia, Pennsylvania: Pennsylvania German Society, 1953.

Klees, Fredric. *The Pennsylvania Dutch.* New York: The Macmillan Company, 1968.

Mitchell, Edwin Valentine. *It's an Old Pennsylvania Custom.* New York: The Vanguard Press, Incorporated, 1947.

Robacker, Earl F. *Pennsylvania Dutch Stuff.* New York: Bonanza Books, 1944.

Stoudt, John Joseph. *Sunbonnets and Shoofly Pies.* New York: Castle Books, 1973.

PRICE GUIDE

Butterfly

Coffeepot, 11"	$4,000.00
Creamer	$900.00
Cup Plate	$800.00
Cup and Saucer, butterfly on the side	$750.00
Cup and Saucer, butterfly in the center	$950.00
Cup and Saucer, cup has rim chip	$500.00
Cup and Saucer, butterfly pattern on the side of the cup and saucer, imperfect	$525.00
Pitcher, milk, 4", mint	$825.00
Plate, 6⅜"	$575.00
Plate, 7¼", butterfly on the side, mint	$750.00
Plate, 8", butterfly on the side, mint	$800.00
Plate, 8¼", butterfly on the side, mint	$900.00
Plate, 8⅜", butterfly on the side, mint	$900.00
Plate, 9¾", mint	$1,500.00
Plate, 9⅞", butterfly in the center, unusual wide spread decoration, mint	$1,700.00
Rare cream pitcher, mint	$1,500.00
Rare plate, 8⅜", proof	$1,250.00
Sugar Bowl	$1,700.00
Teapot	$2,300.00
Waste Bowl	$1,350.00

Carnation

Coffeepot	$1,300.00
Cream Pitcher, 4⅛" high	$800.00
Cup Plate	$650.00
Cup and Saucer, mint	$650.00
Deep Plate, 10", small feather border	$775.00
Deep Plate, 10", large yellow dot border	$750.00
Plate, 7¼", mint	$550.00
Plate, 8"	$600.00
Plate, 8⅜", faint wear	$500.00
Plate, 8⅜", mint	$775.00
Plate, 9¾", small feather border	$975.00
Plate, 9¾", large yellow dot border, mint	$950.00
Soup Plate, 8½"	$700.00
Sugar Bowl	$800.00
Teapot, rare, mint	$7,500.00
Teapot	$1,350.00
Two Cups and Saucers, one age marked	$775.00

Dahlia

Creamer	$900.00
Plate, 8"	$800.00
Plate, 8⅜"	$900.00
Sugar Bowl	$900.00
Tea Bowl and Saucer	$750.00

Double Rose

Creamer	$600.00
Cup Plate	$700.00
Cup and Saucer	$525.00

Double Rose (continued)

Deep Plate, 9¾", hairline	$290.00
Deep Plate, 9¾", mint	$775.00
Plate, 8¾"	$650.00
Plate, 9", mint	$900.00
Plate, 10", mint	$1,000.00
Sugar Bowl	$800.00
Teapot	$725.00
Three-piece tea set, proof creamer, proof sugar bowl with lion handles and covered teapot, mint	$4,500.00
Toddy Plate, 4½", rare	$750.00
Toddy Plate, 5¼", few leaf flakes, rare	$400.00
Two Plates, 7⅝" and 8¼", slightly worn	$525.00
Very Rare Platter, 10½", slightly mellowed, otherwise mint	$2,700.00
Very Rare Platter, 11½", slight mellowing, otherwise mint	$2,950.00
Waste Bowl, 5" diameter, slight mellowing, rare	$275.00
Waste Bowl, 6", mint	$625.00

Dove

Covered Teapot, small flake chips at the spout	$800.00
Creamer	$700.00
Cup and Saucer, plain and broken band, mint	$485.00
Cup and Saucer, blue band, mint	$560.00
Helmet Creamer, rare	$1,275.00
Plate, 6¼", plain border, mint	$500.00
Plate, 6⅜", mint	$500.00
Plate, 8⅛", blue band, mint	$590.00
Plate, 9¾"	$800.00
Sugar Bowl, imperfect cover	$250.00
Teapot, rare, imperfect	$315.00
Teapot	$1,000.00
Toddy Plate	$700.00
Waste Bowl	$700.00

Grape

Cream Pitcher, mint	$695.00
Cup Plate	$600.00
Cup and Saucer	$475.00
Deep Soup, 9¾", slight discoloration	$425.00
Plate, 6", mint	$285.00
Plate, 6¼", mint	$300.00
Plate, 6⅜"	$375.00
Plate, 7", mint	$400.00
Plate, 7⅛", mint	$425.00
Plate, 8", mint	$500.00
Plate, 8¼"	$525.00
Plate, 9¾"	$600.00
Platter, 15"	$900.00
Soup Plate, 8¾"	$450.00
Teapot	$700.00

Grape (continued)
Toddy Plate, 4½" $375.00
Waste Bowl $400.00

Leaf
Bowl, 8¾", unusual shape $1,000.00
Sugar Bowl, covered, mint $1,000.00
Tea Bowl and Saucer $800.00

No Name
Plate, 8½" $400.00

Oyster
Creamer $400.00
Cup and Saucer, both have age marks $285.00
Orange Coffeepot, extremely rare,
    repaired spout $1,250.00
Orange Covered Sugar Bowl, mint condition $1,225.00
Orange Helmet Creamer, chip on the spout $825.00
Plate, 5⅝" $385.00
Plate, 6⅜" $400.00
Plate, 8½" $475.00
Plate, 9¾", orange pattern, mint $1,300.00
Teapot $500.00
Waste Bowl, 6¼", mint $1,100.00

Primrose
Plate, 8¾", impressed "RILEY" $550.00
Sugar Bowl $900.00
Tea Bowl and Saucer $700.00
Waste Bowl $750.00

Single Rose
Coffeepot $725.00
Coffeepot, dome cover, finial repaired,
    few minor chips $1,375.00
Creamer, mint $875.00
Cup Plate $400.00
Cup and Saucer $475.00
Deep Plate, 8¼", mint $400.00
Oblong Sugar Bowl, shell handles, mint $750.00
Plate, 5¼", mint $375.00
Plate, 6¼", mint $425.00
Plate, 6½", mint $450.00
Plate, 6⅜", mint $475.00
Plate, 7¼", mint $500.00
Plate, 9½" $550.00
Plate, unusual, 9¾", bud dot with single line,
    mint, "RILEY" $1,125.00
Soup Plate $375.00
Sugar Bowl, covered $650.00
Tea Bowl and Saucer $300.00
Teapot, mint $1,500.00
Teapot, repaired spout and age marks $550.00
Waste Bowl, 6⅛" diameter $550.00

Strawflower
Plate, 8¼", marked "RILEY,"
    faint spider mark $800.00
Plate, 8½" $825.00
Plate, 9¼" $875.00
Plate, 10", slightly mellowed, marked "RILEY" $925.00
Plate, 10", mint, marked "RILEY" $1,900.00
Soup Plate $800.00
Toddy Plate, 4¾", rim chip, "RILEY" $525.00

Sunflower
Covered Sugar Bowl, rare, lidded, chips $550.00
Creamer $450.00
Plate, 7½", mint $550.00
Plate, 8¼", mint $600.00
Tea Bowl and Saucer $800.00
Two Cups and Saucers, one with an age mark $700.00

Urn
Creamer $350.00
Cup Plate $425.00
Cup and Saucer, mint $445.00
Plate, 7¼", slight discoloration $500.00
Plate, 8¼", mint $625.00
Soup Plate, 8⅞" $500.00
Toddy Plate, rare, 5¼", cracked $250.00
Toddy Plate, rare, 5¼", mint $750.00
Teapot $600.00
Waste Bowl, 5½" diameter, mint $825.00

War Bonnet
Coffeepot, repaired with rivets $900.00
Covered Sugar Bowl, rare, one handle repaired ... $850.00
Creamer $600.00
Cup Plate $650.00
Cup and Saucer,
    slight imperfection on the saucer $685.00
Plate, 6⅜" $575.00
Plate, 8", mint $650.00
Shallow Plate, 8⅛", mint $875.00
Soup Plate $700.00
Teapot, rare, mint condition $2,100.00
Toddy Plate, 5³⁄₁₆", mint $950.00
Toddy Plate, 5¼", shows wear $250.00
Toddy Plate, 5¼", very faint mark $485.00
Toddy Plate, 6", mint $625.00
Toddy Plate, 8" $800.00
Waste Bowl, 5" diameter, mint $1,000.00

Zinnia
Deep Plate, 9¾" $1,125.00
Plate, 6⅜" $600.00
Plate, 8⅜", slight wear on the leaves $750.00

Cybis
Toddy Plate, central butterfly between sprays,
    impressed "CYBIS" $135.00
Cup plate, butterfly to the side, not marked $150.00

IN RETROSPECT

Sam Laidacker was a publisher, writer, collector, and dealer in fine antiques for many years. Today he is considered to be a pathfinder in the field of china. His *Standard Catalogue of Anglo-American China* is one of the best references available as is his publication titled *The American Antiques Collector*. Over the years he worked, researched, and published from his home in Bristol, Pennsylvania.

I was privileged and honored to meet and know Mr. Laidacker when he relocated in later life to a lovely Victorian home in Bloomsburg, Pennsylvania. On many occasions I visited Mr. Laidacker at his home and listened to his sagacious comments on assorted antique subjects.

He taught me a great deal, and with his passing a few years ago, I felt that I had lost a true friend. I acknowledge my indebtedness to him and salute the tremendous wisdom and fortitude that he possessed.

Included here for your inspection is an interesting and worthwhile article researched and written by Mr. Laidacker in the spring of 1949. It appeared in *The American Antiques Collector*, Volume III, Number 7. Note the patterns pictured and the information volunteered, but be especially aware of the prices that were being generated for Gaudy Dutch at leading auction houses during a period from June 1944 through January 1949.

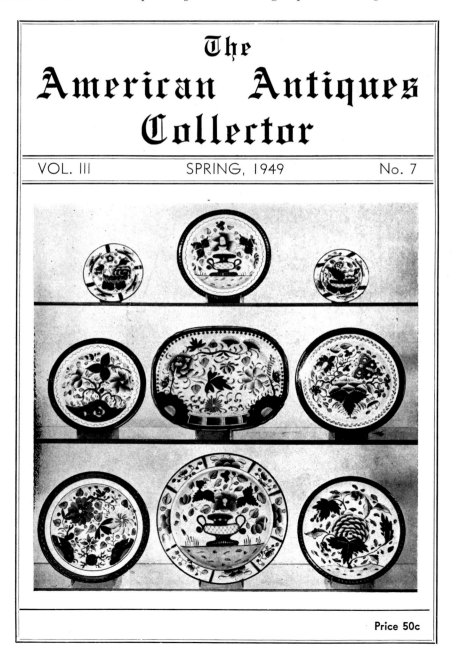

The
American Antiques Collector

VOL. III   SPRING, 1949   No. 7

Price 50c

GAUDY DUTCH

War Bonnet	Single Rose	Strawflower	Carnation
Urn	Grape		Primrose
Carnation	Single Rose		Carnation

IT is quite probable that, in the almost limitless range of English pottery, more superlatives could be used in describing this beautiful ware and telling about collectors' keen rivalry for it than any other category produced by those master potters in the past three centuries. It is beautiful there is no doubt about it. Most everyone desires it, many collect it but no one would have hazarded a guess that a single article would bring as much as $3000 let alone more than twice that amount when the right fabulous price of $6100 was paid for a Butterfly bowl at the Reed sale last October.

Just what is Gaudy Dutch? At the Reed sale I overheard a woman ask a gentleman what is was and he replied, "that it was made in Holland; sent to China to be decorated; thence to England whose merchants sold it here in America, principally to the Dutch". That is just about as far from the truth as it could be. Actually, it was made in England during the first quarter of the 19th century and most of it was exported to the American trade for diligent search has revealed little of it in the home country. As far back as 1939 I had importers trying to find it for me in England.

Oyster

The late Harry Koopman brought me three War Bonnet plates and that was all. Others whom I had searching in England and on the continent had no success.

There are fifteen regular patterns with variations in some of them. There are three distinct types of Butterfly and two of the Urn pattern. The Oyster is found occasionally with a blue transfer border. I've seen articles with that border with an all-over transfer design and it is a Chinese garden scene. In addition to types there are variants of the same pattern accounted for by the fact that a number of different artists were employed to do the decorating. Note the three different Carnation plates shown on these pages. I have record of fourteen different script numbers under the 2/1037 on the War Bonnet pattern. They are i, ii. x, t, y, etc. and the design is consistent on various articles with the same letter. Note how the solid blue lines in the border of the two small plates shown on the cover are different. Those in the one on the left are on a radius, in the one on the right at a tangent. In the same illustration you can see the two types of the Urn pattern. The rare solid border is on the top tier and the generally found and more popular sectional border in the lower tier. The left plate on the lower tier is a newly illustrated pattern called Zinnia. On the right is the Grape.

All of the names are without authority and some of them without reason. The Dove pattern is called Love Bird by some and Spider by others. In this pattern as with most others when the design is used on a hollow piece, part of the design is used on one side and the balance on the other side. Carnation, Double Rose, Primrose, Sunflower and Dahlia are often confused but the differences are soon noted by one who has had the opportunity to examine a lot of Gaudy Dutch. There are many inconsistencies in almost every contact with this beautiful pottery. One collector suggested Scotsman's Hat as a more appropriate name for the pattern called War Bonnet or Indian Bonnet. The later name seems to have been dropped from general use at this writing. I guess that one name would be as good as another and prices would still be erratic.

After discussing it with ceramic authorities the best conclusion that I can draw is that it is a pottery imitation of the so-called and widely term Imari decorated porcelain such as Worcester Imari; Bloor Derby; Crown Derby and Mason's Ironstone made in the period 1780-1820 in England. The brilliant colors are the same except that Gaudy Dutch has a red rim where the fine porcelains have a gilt rim. The blue alone is under the glaze and there is no luster (except on some articles of the Leaf pattern). The attractive colors seem to have a softer effect on pottery than on porcelain which scratches while the top of glaze colors will chip off on the pottery. Pottery cracks easily too. Those are reasons that make it difficult to find proof pieces of Gaudy Dutch and you will note a very wide difference in the prices realized for damaged and proof items.

In the Few-Chrystie sale held by Parke-Bernet in January, 1949 lots 389, 390 and 391 there was sold a large set of Ironstone with the same pattern as that called War Bonnet. The center was the same but the border was sprays of flowers. It was catalogued as "Ironstone China Imari-Pattern circa 1825". I rather suspect that it was made ten years earlier than that for each piece bore the script number 995 and extra letters as those on Gaudy Dutch Ware Bonnet and applied in the same manner. There were over 130 pieces consisting of all size plates, platters, entree dishes, tureens, stands and odd shaped open and covered dishes with most of them marked by means of a blue transfer either "Ironstone China" or "Stone China" in a double lined rectangle along with the number and letters mentioned above. I didn't wait to see it sold but doubt if it brought very much for it was not illustrated and the similarity to Gaudy Dutch was not noted. Quite a lot of the Imari decorated china finds it way into the New York auction market and prices realized are generally nominal and that means that a whole stack of plates— generally proof— will not bring as much as a single piece of the ware that we call Gaudy Dutch. I have seen the War Bonnet design in green transfer decoration so that feather-like decoration was used in different periods.

The name found most frequently on Gaudy Dutch is Riley and it occurs on a number of patterns. Note in the five year cumulative auction records the four 8⅛" Single Rose plates in the Reed sale bearing the Riley imprint. I know of some Single Rose pieces marked Wood. The latest Gaudy Dutch marked pieces that interested me are owned by John Flynn. They are six straight sides cups and four saucers in the Grape pattern. Neither cups or saucers bear the usual script 2/1036 but the saucers bear the circular eagle "Enoch Wood & Sons" impressed mark. Arthur Sussel informs me that he has some pieces in the same pattern with the same mark. Those mentioned are the first I have seen. The fact that these marked pieces do not bear the script number leads me to suspect that several potters made the Grape pattern. Many facts indicate that Gaudy Dutch was made in the period 1800-1825 by a number of makers. From the facts that have been piling up I feel certain that it is but a matter of time before we will know most of its history and origin.

Dahlia

The first article about Gaudy Dutch that appeared in AAC was in Volume I No. 4 where I mentioned the first inquiry about this ware sent to Antiques Magazine before 1930. A whole cupboard-full was shown with the inquiry. I felt sure that someday I would learn to whom that collection belonged and I did find that out in 1944 while doing some appraisal work for Parke-Bernet. It was a collection acquired with more perseverance than money by Parke Edwards and C. Paul Ray. After some collectors and dealers passed up the Edwards-Ray collection, Ira Reed bought it in about

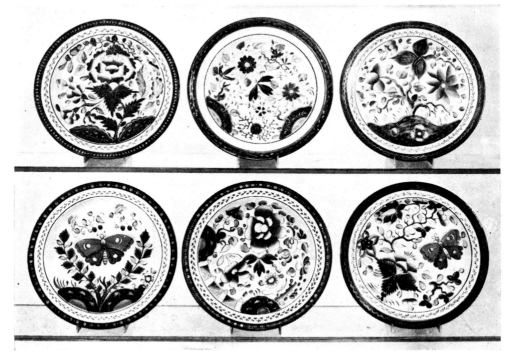

Carnation   Zinnia   Sunflower
Butterfly   Single Rose   Butterfly

1945. It contained many of the items sold in Ira's sale as well as the Butterfly bowl. Some items in the Reed sale came from the Lorimer collection as you can see if you study the records in AAC and examine the illustrations in the Lorimer catalogues and the Reed circular. I talked with Mr. Ray right after the bowl was sold to Mrs. Mabel Renner for $6100 and he told me that he bought it from Gus Pennypacker in about 1925 for $35. During the sale it was referred to as a fruit bowl but the next day Arthur Sussel showed a photograph of a group of pitchers he had owned in 1925 and among them was a Butterfly pitcher with wide lip and flat base, undoubtedly made to go with this bowl. It was slightly discolored and he had sold it in 1925 for $40. If one were to take guesses on the value of that pitcher today the figures would vary greatly.

The prices of all of the items shown on the cover are given in the records in this issue of AAC. Names of the pattern are:—top: War Bonnet on each side and 811b Urn in the middle; middle: Sunflower, Double Rose and 801a Butterfly; bottom: Zinnia; 811a Urn and Grape. The illustration is from Lorimer Part II catalogue. Other illustrations are captioned. You will find the records for items from Lorimer Part I catalogue in the Second Auction Supplement 1938-1944.

More about Gaudy Dutch as well as Spatter, King's Rose, luster of all kinds, etc., etc., will be found in my coming book about decoration on pottery and porcelain for the American trade. The key letters used in that section of Auction Supplement III published in this issue of AAC are as follows: LII Lorimer Part II, New York 10/24-27/44; HV Haskell Part

GAUDY DUTCH

SPRING, 1949   183

| *Dove* | *Grape* | *Urn* |

V. New York 12/8/44; Ho Ida Hostetter, Lancaster, Pa., 10/16 and 11/20/46; U Earl Unger, Reading, Pa. 11/27/47; He Hess Bros., Allentown, Pa. 12/30/46; WS Wharton Sinkler, Reading, Pa. 11/27/47; St J. Stogdell Stokes, New York 3/20/48 and Rd Ira Reed, Reading, Pa. 10/27/48. It is quite likely that Auction Supplement III will be ready for delivery by the time this issue of AAC reaches you. It is suggested that collectors and dealers study the condensed auction records with a great deal of thought. Notice the consistently wide gap in prices for proof and defective items. One of the best illustrations is in the Reed sale where four hollow pieces in the Grape pattern brought $180 each and sold right after them was a sugar bowl with a slight crack that brought but $40. Close observation will disclose many similar occurences. There is much more to be written about this beautiful pottery.

Prices realized in leading auction houses for Gaudy Dutch sold during the period June. 1944 through January, 1949.

801 Butterfly
  a. Butterfly at side. Wide border band.
  b. Butterfly in border. Narrow border band.
  c. Butterfly in center between two sprays. Two loops at base.

801a Butterfly—wide border band
  14″ bowl Rd $6100.00
  Cup plate Rd rpd $70
  Cup and saucer LII601 five cups and six saucers (three cups disc) $110; Ho $80; Rd set of six $510
  9⅞″ plate LII708 disc $130; Ho $250; Rd disc $130
  9¾″ soup plate Rd $180
  8½″ plate LII599 $90; LII691 $70
  8¼″ soup plate U19 (LI671) two for $200
  8″ plate Rd disc $85
  7½″ plate LII597 $90; LII707 $110
  7″ plate He wrn $65
  6½″ plate Rd $150
  6″ deep plate Rd $77.50
  6″ plate Rd $150
  Teapot LII602 spout chp $170

801b Butterfly—narrow border band
  Teapot U19 (LI673) $550; U19 (LI674) $275
  10″ plate LII709 flakes on top $40; Rd slightly mellow $185
  8″ plate St 31 wrn $55
801c Butterfly—between sprays
  Cup and saucer LII600 three for $210; WS $62.50
  Cup WS $25
  10″ plate LII705 $220; LII706 $210 Ho $250; St26 $160; Rd $220
  8½″ plate LII598 $170
  7½″ plate WS $85; Rd two for $280
  6″ plate Rd two for $280
802 Carnation
  6″ bowl Rd $100
  Cup and Saucer Ho $55; Ho $35; St23 two-one crk $65; WS $42.50; Rd two for $120; Rd crk $47.50
  Teapot LII603 $210
  9¾″ plate LII703 $150; U28 $150; Ws wrn $30; WS $47.50; Rd $180
  8½″ plate LII700 slight twist $40; U28 $100; U28 $75
  8″ plate K2 3 4 three $150; Rd four for $210

77

7½" **plate** LII699 two (one disc) $40; He34 $22.50; WS two for $100

7¼" **plate** U28 two for $150

7" **plate** Rd seven for $385

5" **plate** WS wrn $45; Rd not prf $27.50

803   Dahlia

Creamer Rd $90

9" **plate** Rd 95

8⅛" **plate** St19 with 8" Zinnia plate $70

804   Double Rose

Cup and saucer U28 two for $120

Cup plate Rd $90

10" **plate** WS abt prf $70; WS two not prf $45

9¾" **soup plate** LII606 two-disc-chp $35; WS $45;

9" **soup plate** Rd $80

Teapot WS abt prf $160; Rd $220

8½" **soup plate** WS disc $22.50

8¼" **plate** LII607 two, one disc-one chp $40

7" **plate** Ho wrn $22.50

6¼" **plate** He22 $30

5¼" **plate** U28 $105

5" **plate** WS $70

17" **platter** U18 (LI538) $1600

10½" **platter** LII690 slightly mellow $325

LII602 7¾" and 7¼" plate-scaled $40

805   Dove

Bowl 5" Rd two for $130

12" **coffee pot** Rd $240

Creamer-tall Rd $110

Cup and saucer Ho $45; WS two (abt prf) $55; WS three dmg $30; Rd three for $135; Rd cup crk $25

10" **plate** Ho $120; Ho crk $42.50; WS dmg $22.50; Rd $140

806   Grape

4½" **cup plate** Rd two for $300; Rd disc $35

3½" **cup plate** Ho mended $70; Rd two for $370

Straight side cup and saucer LII595 two for $60; U23 chp $47.50; WS $25; Rd set of six $375; Rd $33

Creamer, sugar bowl and two sized teapots Rd $720

Sugar bowl Rd slight crk $40

9¾" **plate** U24 two for $280; WS two wrn $65; St30 crk with 8¼" $95; Rd two for $260

10" **soup plate** U23 two for $170; WS wrn $32.50

9" **plate** U24 $65; Rd $52.50

8½" **plate** WS two for $75; Rd $45

8¼" **plate** St30 with 9¾" crk $95

8" **plate** LII684 three for $110; Ho $60; WS two wrn $36; Rd three for $150

7½" **plate** Ho wrn $40

7¼" **plate** LII696 three disc $60

7" **plate** LII608 $30; LII609 $50; LII698 three for $75; WS four for $130; WS two disc and chp $30; Rd three for $135

7" **deep plate** Rd $65

5½" **plate** LII593 $40; He44 $65

5¼" **plate** LII594 two-slight chps $70; Ho wrn $40

5" **plate** Rd $55; Rd not prf $27.50 LII683 6¼" plate and cup and saucer $35

807   Oyster

5½" **bowl** LII682 chp $25; WS $82.50; Rd crk $60

Cup and saucer LII590 set of six-yellow-ground $170; LII694 set of five-yellow ground-few defects $60; LII695 set of four-yellow ground $55; U27 $60; He84 $28; WS two for $85; WS two for $70; Rd set of six $435; Rd $37

Creamer, sugar bowl and teapot Rd $570

10" **plate** Ho rim chp $80; Ho crk $40; U27 three for $480; U27 chp $50

9" **plate** Rd four for $160

8⅛" **plate** LII588 apricot ground $110; LII697 two-wrn-apricot ground $35; WS three for $120

7" **plate** Rd two for $100

6½" **plate** Rd $31

808   Primrose

8⅜" **plate** St29 $45

809   Single Rose

6½" **bowl** Rd $85

5" **bowl** Rd two for $310

Coffee pot LII604 slight rpr $185; WS rpd and made up cover $95

Creamer U27 $100

Sugar bowl He86 crk $26

Teapot Rd 6" round $155; Rd 5½" round $155

Cup and saucer round LII584 three for $55; LII586 set of six $100; Ho rpd $35; U26 three for $130; He39-43 set of five (3 crks) $130; WS set of six $210; WS disc $15; St24 four for $90; Rd set of six $420; Rd set of four $160; Rd $32.50

10" **plate** Ho crk $42.50; He 38 crk $22.50; WS $70; WS dmg $30; St28 abt prf $70; Rd $100; Rd $100; Rd $90; Rd $82.50; Rd $65

10" **soup plate** LII701 $50; U29 $90; WS $60

9" **plate** WS dmg $22.50

8¼" **plate** U29 $40

8½" **plate** WS three for $120

8⅛" **plate** Rd set of six (four impressed RILEY) $330

7½" **plate** He27-32 set of six-two wrn $179

7¼" **plate** LII610 two for $50

7" plate Rd disc $35
6⅜" plate LII592 two for $60
6" plate Ho six-wrn and crk $66
5⅜" plate HV497 set of six $260
LII591 6½" bowl crk and two cups (one with handle) $30; LII613 10" plate crk and soup plate scaled $40

810   Sunflower
6¼" bowl LII596 $80
Cup and saucer U26 three for $180; WS set of six $225; Rd set of six $390
10" plate LII702 abt prf $65; WS $87.50; WS $80
8½" plate WS two for $90
8¼" plate U25 two for $140
8" plate Rd $45
7½" plate LII689 three for $110; WS two disc $50
7¼" plate U25 and U29 three for $150
7" plate Rd two for $88

811   Urn
a.   Sectional border
b.   Solid border

811a   Urn-sectional border
Cup and saucer-round Ho rpd $50; U22 $65; U22 crk $30; WS set of four $160; St25 four, some scaled and 8" plate crk $150; Rd set of four $260
Cup and saucer-ridge side WS $40; WS chp $15
Coffee pot Ho rpd $140; Rd 11½" $575
4¼" cup plate Rd crk $130
10" plate LII612 rim chp and wrn $20; LII688 disc $80; U22 $160
8¼" plate LII611 two for $140; U22 $110; WS $50; Rd $75; Rd $45; Rd rpd $25
8¼" soup plate He $45
7½" plate U29 $110
7" plate He25, 26 $100; He $42.50
6" plate WS crk and disc $30

811b   Urn-solid border
7¼" plate LII687 $60; WS $40

812   War Bonnet
6" bowl Rd $150
4¾" cup plate LII686 $90; Rd crk $70
4¼" cup plate LII685 $130
Cup and saucer-straight side U21 $60; WS two for $90
Cup and saucer-round LII585 two for $65
10" plate He36, 37 two for $130
10" soup plate U21 (Y746) three for $315; Rd two for $320
9" plate Rd disc $72.50
9" soup plate Rd $120
8½" soup plate WS two for $65; WS wrn $27.50
8" plate U20 five for $375; WS five for $337.50; WS wrn $27.50
7" plate He24 rim chp $25
7" soup plate U21 $65; Rd $80
6" plate LII589 $70
5" plate Rd crk $80
LII587 5¼" plate prf and 4⅝" plate scaled on back $80

813   Strawflower (impressed RILEY)
10" plate U22 $250
8½" plate Rd $65

814   Zinnia (impressed RILEY)
10" plate Rd $75
10" soup plate LII704 $140
9" plate Rd $80
8⅜" plate LII692 $70; LII693 two almost prf $100
8" plate St19 with 8¼" Dahlia $70

815   Leaf
6" plate Rd $65

LII710 Single Rose small plate, Urn and Dahlia cups and Carnation cup and saucer-defects $45; LII711 Oyster cup and saucer prf, two Butterfly saucers, Oyster, Grape and Double Rose plates and an Oyster plate with blue transfer border. Some defects $50

Sam Laidacker wrote from his Bristol, Pennsylvania home reporting that "the action of Gaudy Dutch is bewildering. It was a short time ago that a few hundred dollars was a big price for a single item. Now . . . !"

"A few years ago it would have been impossible to perceive the scope of the study of American history as portrayed by the English potters. Now, as we can see it clearly, the study has no limit when we consider the historical association of the view depicted, the artist who was responsible for the original drawing or painting, the publication in which it first appeared in printed form before being adapted by the potters, and, knowledge of the potter and when and where he worked and something about the workmen."

In May 1938, Mr. Laidacker set out on the arduous task of making a record of the historical and decorative Staffordshire made from about 1810 to 1850 for the American trade and sold in the principal auction rooms of the United States. His first supplement closed with June 1944 and was compiled from auction catalogues and reports to include American Views Series, Decorative Series, Dark Blue Historical, Landing of Lafayette, The States of America and Independence Series, Historical and Literary Views, Doctor Syntax Series, Wilkie Series, Picturesque Views/Hudson River Series, The Arms Series, American City Series, Flower and Scroll Border, Floral Border, Eagle and Scroll Border, Irregular Borders, Regular Borders, Miscellaneous Views on Dark Blue, Miscellaneous Views/Light Colors, Gaudy Dutch, Spatter, and Salopian.

The second auction supplement took on the same form and dealt with a listing of sales generated for the period from June 1944 through and including January 1949. Much new and helpful information was presented including additional photographs, conditions, and prices generated for assorted Gaudy Dutch shapes, Spatter, King's Rose pattern 833, Shell King's Rose, Single Rose, Cabbage Rose, Basket of Roses, Strawberry, and others.

Pertinent information contributing to this study has been included in its entirety as it originally appeared when Mr. Laidacker first presented his findings. You will note that many subjects are illustrated, listing their pattern, lot number, shape, condition, size, price, and the collection where the example originated.

AUCTION SUPPLEMENT

To

THE
STANDARD CATALOGUE

Of

ANGLO-AMERICAN CHINA
FROM 1810 TO 1850

A RECORD OF HISTORICAL AND DECORATIVE STAFFORDSHIRE
MADE ORIGINALLY FOR THE AMERICAN TRADE
AND SOLD IN THE PRINCIPAL AUCTION
ROOMS OF THE UNITED STATES

DURING THE PERIOD
FROM MAY, 1938 TO JUNE, 1944

COMPILED FROM THE AUCTION
CATALOGUES AND REPORTS

1944

COMPILED AND PUBLISHED BY
SAM LAIDACKER
316 N. WASHINGTON AVE., SCRANTON 1, PA.

CHRONOLOGICAL LIST OF COLLECTIONS SOLD
AS REPORTED IN THIS COMPILATION

HIII MRS. J. AMORY HASKELL
Part III of a collection of lighter colors and dark blue historical views sold by Parke-Bernet Galleries, New York, October 11 and 12, 1944.

LII GEORGE HORACE LORIMER
Part II of an extensive collection of dark blue historictl views, Gaudy Dutch and Spatter sold by Parke-Bernet Galleries, New York, October 24, 25, 26 and 27, 1944.

HIV MRS. J. AMORY HASKELL
Part IV of a collection of lighter colors and dark blue historical views sold by Parke-Bernet Galleries, November 8 and 9, 1944.

HV MRS. J. AMORY HASKELL
Part V of a collection of gaudily decorated and lighter colors and dark blue historical views sold by Parke-Bernet Galleries, New York, December 7 and 8, 1944.

Sm HERSCHEL G. SMITH
Collection of dark blue and lighter colors historical views sold by Wm. D. Morley, Inc., Philadelphia, Pa., January 22, 1945.

HVI MRS. J. AMORY HASKELL
Part VI of a collection of Gaudy Dutch, gaudily decorated and lighter color and dark blue historical views sold by Parke-Bernet Galleries, New York, February 13 and 14, 1945.

Mi I. HAZLETON MIRKIL
Collection of lighter colors and dark blue historical views sold by Samuel T. Freeman & Co., Philadelphia, Pa., February 15, 1945.

Gi HARROLD E. GILLINGHAM
Collection of dark blue historical and literary subjects sold by Samuel T. Freeman & Co., Philadelphia, Pa., April 17, 1945.

Ho MRS. IDA K. HOSTETTER
Collection of Gaudy Dutch and historical subjects sold by Reed-Pennypacker-Kleinfelter, Lancaster, Pa., October 16 and November 20, 1946.

B MAURICE BRIX
Collection of dark blue and lighter colors historical views sold by Samuel T. Freeman & Co., Philadelphia, Pa., November 7, 1946.

U EARL and LUCY UNGER
Collection of dark blue historical views and Gaudy Dutch sold by Pennypacker-Kleinfelter, Reading, Pa., November 27, 1946.

He HESS BROTHERS
Collection of historical dark blue views, Gaudy Dutch, Spatter and King's Rose sold by S. W. Queen, Allentown, Pa., December 30, 1946.

PW MRS. PERCY WILLIAMSON
Collection of historical ark bldue views and King's Rose sold by Pennypacker-Kleinfelter, Pottstown, Pa., February 5, 1947.

HI MRS. AMORY HASKELL
Part I of a collection of dark blue historical views sold by Parke-Bernet Galleries, Inc., in New York, N. Y., April 26, 1944.

HII MRS. J. AMORY HASKELL
Part II of a collection lighter color Hudson River and other views and dark blue views sold by Parke-Bernet Galleries, Inc., in New York, N. Y., May 17 and 18, 1944.

And a number of smaller collections.

Sh—Sheldon; Bl—Blight; GW—George Wisecarver.

GAUDY DUTCH

Gaudy Dutch

801 Butterfly

a. Butterfly at side. Wide border band.

b. Butterfly in border. Narrow border band.

c. Butterfly in center between two sprays. Two loops at base.

801a Butterfly—wide border band

Cup and saucer Y715 two (slight wear) $55; LI518 three (not proof) $55; LI676 four matching (one saucer crk.) $210

97⁄8″ **plate** LI675 $150
81⁄4″ **plate** Wi922 $30

81⁄4″ **soup plate** LI671 two for $110
71⁄2″ **plate** Y700 $67.50; LI678 two for $150

61⁄2″ **plate** LI679 two for $120

53⁄4″ **plate** LI677 $90

801b Butterfly—narrow border band

Coffee pot Y716 (cover of another pattern) $375
Teapot LI673 about proof $140; LI674 slight defects $110
10″ **plate** LI672 $125

801c Butterfly—between sprays
Cup and saucer Y714 set of six matching (one cup cracked) $275

801 *Butterfly*

802 Carnation

93⁄4″ **plate** LI521 two for $180

81⁄4″ **plate** Y698 $32.50; Wi921 (worn) $17.50
71⁄2″ **plate** LI669 two for $75

63⁄8″ **plate** Y713 $32.50; LI540 two (almost proof) $30
Round bowl—61⁄2″ Y721 $70; LI527 $50

802 Carnation

Round creamer—41⁄2″ Y722 $67.50

Round teapot—61⁄2″ Y719 $140

Cup and saucer-round Y720 two for $40; LI517 two (crk) $25

Cup and saucer-median ridge LI682 two for $60

Gaudy Dutch—(continued)

saucer and bowl $22.50; Wi926 teapot $30; LI665 three 8⅜" plates and two saucers (worn) $50

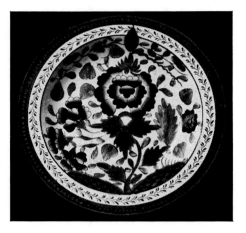

802   Carnation

803   Dahlia
   Creamer Wi917 $20
   Teapot Y702 $40
   8⅛" plate Y701 $35

804   Double Rose
   10" plate Wi930 (rim chip) $22.50

   9¾" soup plate LI670 $85
   7¾" plate Wi923 three for $55

   17" platter LI528 $520
   Cup and saucer Y695 two for $35; Du 284 set of six (one crk) $75
   Y762 7¾" plate and 9¾" soup plate (each disc.) $35; Wi 918 cup,

805   Dove
   9¾" plate Y733 two for $180
   11" coffee pot Wi925 (chip on spout) $65
   Round cup and saucer Y718 set of six $120; LI667 three cups and five saucers $90

   Y717 sugar bowl, tea pot, low creamer and round creamer $175
   Round bowl—5¾" Wi915 (crk) $20

806   Grape
   4½" cup plate Wi913 $40

   3½" cup plate Y706 $90; Y738 two (one crk) $110; LI541 four 3½" to 4½"—only one proof $120

   Straight side cup and saucer Wi916 four for $40; LI531 two for $45; LI534 two—not matching $30

   9¾" plate Wi933 $35; LI533 two for $130

   10" soup plate Y735 two for $75

   8¼" plate Y739 $30; Wi920 $20; LI524 four for $140

   7¼" plate Y737 two for $45

   Y736 7¼", 6¼" and 4½" plates (crk) $40

807   Oyster
   5½" bowl LI515 (chp) $20

   Cup and saucer LI537 three matched $50; LI685 four for $90; LI686 four for $70; LI687 four (not proof) $40

   10" plate LI689 two (one not proof) $85; LI691 two for $180

   8¼" plate LI535 two (not proof) $40; LI688 two for $65; LI690 two (one disc) for $60

   8¼" plate with blue border Y704 $42.50
   7½" plate Y703 $25
   Y705 6¼" bowl (chps), creamer (proof) and sugar bowl (cover rpd) $65; LI684 coffee pot, tea pot, creamer, sugar bowl and waste bowl $450

GAUDY DUTCH

Gaudy Dutch—(continued)

808   Primrose
   4¼″ **cup plate** Y708 $85
   8½″ **plate** LI529 (impressed RILEY)
$55; LI530 (worn) $35
   8⅜″ **plate** Y699 $40
   Saucer LI516 $12.50

810   Sunflower
   5⅝″ **bowl** Y697 disc $35
   8¼″ **plate** LI568 two for $60
   7½″ **plate** LI519 two for $70;
LI520 two—one disc and one rpd $50
Wi919 four cups and three saucers
—not all proof $22.50

807 'Oyster'

809 Single Rose
   6½″ **bowl** Y730 two for $60

   Coffee pot Y723 12″ proof $300;
Y724 11¼″ (Rpd and crk) $80

   Cup and saucer—round Y725 six
matched $140; Y726 six—not matched
$67.50; Wi 929 set of six matched
$50; LI522 five cups and four saucers
$70; LI680 four cups and six saucers
$100

   4⅛″ **cup plate** Y707 two with slight
disc $105
   10″ **plate** Y727 $85; Wi931 (crk)
$15; LI523 two for $140; LI683 two
for $170
   7¾″ **plate** Y731 set of six $115

   7¼″ **plate** LI536 three—two flat
and one deep $70

   6½″ **plate** Y732 five for $180

   Sugar bowl Wi927 (crk) $20
   Teapot Wi924 (Cov rpd) $30
   Y728 5⅜″ and 8⅛″ plates $65;
Y729 bowl and low creamer $180;
LI666 two 6¼″ plates and one 5¼″
$80

811   Urn
   10″ **plate** Y740 two for $210

   7½″ **plate** Y743 two for $70; LI528
two for $120

   Cup and saucer Y741 set of six
$150; LI664 two for $45

   Y742 5¾″ and 6½″ plates $75;
LI681 8″ and 8⅜″ plates (one not
proof) $110; LI542 two 6¼″ plates,

   a 5⅛″ bowl and a crk saucer $45

813   Strawflower (impressed RILEY)
   10″ **plate** Y734 two for $130; Wi932
$37.50

   8½″ **plate** LI668 two for $120

   5½″ **plate** LI526 $50

   LI692 10″ plate (disc) and 4¾″
cup plate (chp) $115

GAUDY DUTCH

Gaudy Dutch—(continued)

813 *'Strawflower'*   812 *'War Bonnet'*   809 *'Single Rose'*

812   War Bonnet

4¼″ **cup plate** Y711 $95

3⅜ **cup plate** Y712 two (crk) $170

9¾″ **plate** Y744 six for $400; Y745 two—not proof $70

9¾″ **soup plate** Y746 three for $120

8⅛″ **plate** Y747 six for $175; Y754 two for $100

8″ **soup plate** Y749 three (mellow) for $120; Y748 three for $140

Cup and saucer-round Y758 six for $240; Y761 two (not proof) $45

Cup and saucer—straight side Y759 four for $230; Y760 four saucers only $50; LI539 three—not matching (one cup crk) $70

7¼″ **plate** Y752 four (one mellow) $110; LI532 two (one worn) for $50

7⅛″ **soup plate** Y753 two for $50

6¼″ **plate** Y751 $45

6″ **plate** Y709 four for $120

5¼″ **plate** Y710 $40

4⅝″ **plate** Y750 three for $150

5¼″ **bowl** LI525 $50

Creamer—low type Y757 (crk) $35

Sugar bowl—rectangular Y756 $80

Teapot Y755 $290

805 *'Dove'*   806 *'Grape'*   811 *'Urn'*

CHRONOLOGICAL LIST OF COLLECTIONS SOLD
AS REPORTED IN THIS COMPILATION

C   MRS. JOHN A. COYLE

Collection of dark blue historical, Doctor Syntax and Don Quixote views sold by L. J. Gilbert & Son in Lancaster, Pa., May 26, 1938.

V   O. P. AND M. J. VAN SWERINGEN

Collection of dark blue historical views sold by Parke-Bernet Galleries, Inc., near Cleveland, Ohio, October 26, 1938.

H   WILLIAM RANDOLPH HEARST

Collection of dark blue and lighter colors historical views sold by Parke-Bernet Galleries, Inc., in New York, N. Y., November 17, 18 and 19, 1938.

F   A PRIVATE COLLECTION

Collection of dark blue historical views sold by Samuel T. Freeman Co., in Philadelphia, Pa., December 13, 1938.

A   A PRIVATE COLLECTION

Collection of dark blue historical views sold by the American Art Association-Anderson Galleries, Inc., in New York, N. Y., April 15, 1939.

Cv   A CLEVELAND, OHIO COLLECTOR

Collection of dark blue and carmine historical and decorative views sold by Parke-Bernet Galleries, Inc., in New York, N. Y., December 13, 1940.

W   C. ERNEST WAGNER

Collection of dark blue historical and literary views sold by L. J. Gilbert & Son in Lancaster, Pa., February 19, 1941.

Y   MRS. MARY MARGARET YEAGER

Collection of dark blue and carmine historical views and Gaudy Dutch with special groups of States, Landing of Lafayette, Adams American views and War Bonnet Gaudy Dutch sold by Parke-Bernet Galleries, Inc., in New York, N. Y., March 18, 19 and 20, 1943.

Du   MRS. J. AUSTIN DU PONT

Collection of dark blue historical views and some Gaudy Dutch sold by Parke-Bernet Galleries, Inc., in New York, N. Y., May 7, 1943.

Wi   MRS. ALICE JONES WILLOCK

Collection of dark blue Staffordshire and Gaudy Dutch sold by Parke-Bernet Galleries, Inc., in New York, N. Y., May 13, 1943.

Se   MRS. THERESE SEMON

Collection of dark blue historical views sold by Kende Galleries in New York, N. Y., June 4, 1943.

Ha   R. T. HAINES HALSEY

Collection of dark blue historical Staffordshire sold by Parke-Bernet Galleries, Inc., in New York, N. Y., November 11 and 12, 1943.

Ca   PHILIP D. CASTNER

Collection of dark blue historical Staffordshire sold by Samuel T. Freeman & Co., in Philadelphia, Pa., December 15, 1943.

Ll   GEORGE HORACE LORIMER

Part I of an extensive collection of dark blue historical views, Gaudy Dutch and Spatter sold by Parke-Bernet Galleries, Inc., in New York, N. Y., March 29, 30, 31 and April, 1, 1944.

Ni NEW YORK EDUCATIONAL INSTITUTION
Literary and historical subjects on dark blue sold by Parke-Bernet Galleries, New York, February 14, 1947.

KD KOUNTZE-DUNNE (Mrs. Francis Garvin)
Collection of Landing of Lafayette and other dark blue subjects sold by Parke-Bernet Galleries, New York, March 13, 1947.

GB W. GRIFFIN GRIBBEL
Collection of dark blue and lighter color historical subjects sold by Wm. D. Morely, Inc., Philadelphia, Pa., April 29, 1947.

K C. A. KLEINFELTER
Collection of dark blue historical, Gaudy Dutch and Spatter sold by Pennypacker-Kleinfelter, Lebanon, Pa., April 17, 1947.

WS WHARTON SINKLER
Collection of Gaudy Dutch and Ridgway "Beauties of America" sold by Pennypacker-Kleinfelter, Reading, Pa., November 27, 1947.

AH ALBERT HAASIS
Collection of dark blue historical and literary subjects sold by Savoy Galleries, New York, February 6, 1948.

St J. STOGDELL STOKES
Collection of Gaudy Dutch sold by Parke-Bernet Galleries, New York, March 20, 1948.

Cr CRAWFORD
Collection of dark blue historical subjects sold by Pennypacker-Kleinfelter, Reading, Pa., June 30, 1948.

BH ANNIE R. BIRD and JOSEPHINE BIRD HALL
Collection of lighter colors and dark blue historical views sold by Parke-Bernet Galleries, New York, October 7, 1948.

Rd IRA S. REED
Collection of Gaudy Dutch sold by Pennypacker-Kleinfelter, Reading, Pa., October 27, 1948.

Ab MARTIN E. ALBERT
Collection of dark blue historical subjects sold by Parke-Bernet Galleries, New York, January 13, 1949.

And items from various smaller collections.

ABBREVIATIONS USED IN THIS COMPILATION

bdr	border	**prf**	proof: fine glaze, clear transfer, good color, no chips, no cracks and a very minimum of wear
chp	chip		
chk	check: an inside crack not reaching to the rim		
crk	crack	**rpd**	repaired: probably several defects repaired
dmgd	damaged: more than one kind of defect	**rpr**	repair: generally a single defect repaired
disc	discolored	**w c**	with cover
n c	no cover	**wrn**	worn

GAUDY DUTCH

801 Butterfly

a. Butterfly at side. Wide border band.

b. Butterfly in border. Narrow border band.

c. Butterfly in center between two sprays. Two loops at base.

801a Butterfly—wide border band

14″ bowl Rd $6100.00

Cup plate Rd rpd $70

Cup and saucer LII601 five cups and six saucers (three cups disc) $110; Ho $80; Rd set of six $510

9⅞″ plate LII708 disc $130; Ho $250; Rd disc $130

9¾″ soup plate Rd $180

8½″ plate LII599 $90; (LI691) $70

8¼″ soup plate U19 (LI671) two for $200

8″ plate Rd disc $85

7½″ plate LII597 $90; LII707 $110

7″ plate He wrn $65

6½″ plate Rd $150

6″ deep plate Rd $77.50

6″ plate Rd $150

Teapot LII602 spout chp $170

		Grape		*Sunflower*		*Butterfly*		*Grape*	
	Carnation			*Butterfly Single Rose*				*Butterfly*	
Top:		593		596		597		595	
Middle:	601			599		598		600	
Bottom:		603				604		602	

GAUDY DUTCH

	War Bonnet	*Urn*	*War Bonnet*
	Sunflower	*Double Rose*	*Butterfly*
	Zinnia	*Urn*	*Grape*

Top:	686	687	685
Middle:	689	690	691
Bottom:	692	688	684

801b Butterfly—narrow border band
 Teapot U19 (LI673) $550; U19 (LI674) $275
 10″ plate LII709 flakes on top $40; Rd slightly mellow $185
 8″ plate St 31 wrn $55

801c Butterfly—between sprays
 Cup and saucer LII600 three for $210; WS $62.50
 Cup WS $25
 10″ plate LII705 $220; LII706 $210 Ho $250; St26 $160; Rd $220
 8½″ plate LII598 $170
 7½″ plate WS $85; Rd two for $280
 6″ plate Rd two for $280

802 Carnation
 6″ bowl Rd $100
 Cup and Saucer Ho $55; Ho $35; St23 two-one crk $65; WS $42.50; Rd two for $120; Rd crk $47.50
 Teapot LII603 $210
 9¾″ plate LII703 $150; U28 $150; Ws wrn $30; WS $47.50; Rd $180
 8½″ plate LII700 slight twist $40; U28 $100; U28 $75
 8″ plate K2 3 4 three $150; Rd four for $210
 7½″ plate LII699 two (one disc) $40; He34 $22.50; WS two for $100
 7¼″ plate U28 two for $150
 7″ plate Rd seven for $385
 5″ plate WS wrn $45; Rd not prf $27.50

803   Dahlia
   Creamer Rd $90
   9″ plate Rd 95
   8⅛″ plate St19 with 8″ Zinnia plate $70

804   Double Rose
   Cup and saucer U28 two for $120
   Cup plate Rd $90
   10″ plate WS abt prf $70; WS two not prf $45
   9¾″ soup plate LI1606 two-disc-chp $35; WS $45;
   9″ soup plate Rd $80
   Teapot WS abt prf $160; Rd $220
   8½″ soup plate WS disc $22.50
   8¼″ plate LI1607 two, one disc-one chp $40
   7″ plate Ho wrn $22.50
   6¼″ plate He22 $30
   5¼″ plate U28 $105
   5″ plate WS $70
   17″ platter U18 (LI538) $1600
   10½″ platter LI1690 slightly mellow $325
   LI1602 7¾″ and 7¼″ plate-scaled $40

805   Dove
   Bowl 5″ Rd two for $130
   12″ coffee pot Rd $240
   Creamer-tall Rd $110
   Cup and saucer Ho $45; WS two (abt prf) $55; WS three dmg $30; Rd three for $135; Rd cup crk $25
   10″ plate Ho $120; Ho crk $42.50; WS dmg $22.50; Rd $140

806   Grape
   4½″ cup plate Rd two for $300; Rd disc $35
   3½″ cup plate Ho mended $70; Rd two for $370
   Straight side cup and saucer LI1595 two for $60; U23 chp $47.50; WS $25; Rd set of six $375; Rd $33
   Creamer, sugar bowl and two sized teapots Rd $720
   Sugar bowl Rd slight crk $40
   9¾″ plate U24 two for $280; WS two wrn $65; St30 crk with 8¼″ $95; Rd two for $260
   10″ soup plate U23 two for $170; WS wrn $32.50
   9″ plate U24 $65; Rd $52.50
   8½″ plate WS two for $75; Rd $45
   8¼″ plate St30 with 9¾″ crk $95
   8″ plate LI1684 three for $110; Ho $60; WS two wrn $36; Rd three for $150
   7½″ plate Ho wrn $40

   7¼″ plate LI1696 three disc $60
   7″ plate LI1608 $30; LI1609 $50; LI1698 three for $75; WS four for $130; WS two disc and chp $30; Rd three for $135
   7″ deep plate Rd $65
   5½″ plate LI1593 $40; He44 $65
   5¼″ plate LI1594 two-slight chps $70; Ho wrn $40
   5″ plate Rd $55; Rd not prf $27.50
   LI1683 6¼″ plate and cup and saucer $35

807   Oyster
   5½″ bowl LI1682 chp $25; WS $82.50; Rd crk $60
   Cup and saucer LI1590 set of six-yellow-ground $170; LI1694 set of five-yellow ground-few defects $60; LI1695 set of four-yellow ground $55; U27 $60; He84 $28; WS two for $85; WS two for $70; Rd set of six $435; Rd $37
   Creamer, sugar bowl and teapot Rd $570
   10″ plate Ho rim chp $80; Ho crk $40; U27 three for $480; U27 chp $50
   9″ plate Rd four for $160
   8⅛″ plate LI1588 apricot ground $110; LI1697 two-wrn-apricot ground $35; WS three for $120
   7″ plate Rd two for $100
   6½″ plate Rd $31

808   Primrose
   8⅜″ plate St29 $45

809   Single Rose
   6½″ bowl Rd $85
   5″ bowl Rd two for $310
   Coffee pot LI1604 slight rpr $185; WS rpd and made up cover $95
   Creamer U27 $100
   Sugar bowl He86 crk $26
   Teapot Rd 6″ round $155; Rd 5½″ round $155
   Cup and saucer round LI1584 three for $55; LI1586 set of six $100; Ho rpd $35; U26 three for $130; He39-43 set of five (3 crks) $130; WS set of six $210; WS disc $15; St24 four for $90; Rd set of six $420; Rd set of four $160; Rd $32.50
   10″ plate Ho crk $42.50; He 38 crk $22.50; WS $70; WS dmg $30; St28 abt prf $70; Rd $100; Rd $100; Rd $90; Rd $82.50; Rd $65
   10″ soup plate LI1701 $50; U29 $90; WS $60
   9″ plate WS dmg $22.50
   8¼″ plate U29 $40
   8½″ plate WS three for $120

GAUDY DUTCH

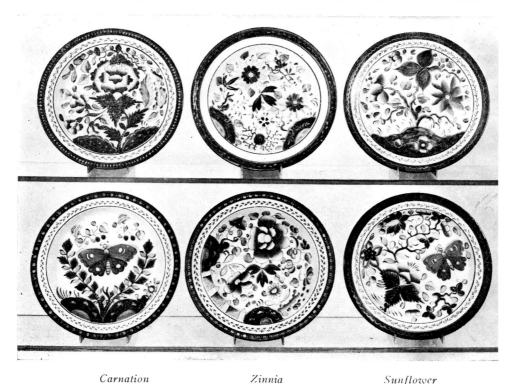

Carnation		Zinnia	Sunflower
Butterfly		*Single Rose*	*Butterfly*
Top:	703	704	702
Bottom:	705	701	708

8⅛″ **plate** Rd set of six (four impressed RILEY) $330
7½″ **plate** He27-32 set of six-two wrn $179
7¼″ **plate** LII610 two for $50
7″ **plate** Rd disc $35
6⅜″ **plate** LII592 two for $60
6″ **plate** Ho six-wrn and crk $66
5⅜″ **plate** HV497 set of six $260
LII591 6½″ bowl crk and two cups (one with handle) $30; LII613 10″ plate crk and soup plate scaled $40

810   Sunflower
6¼″ **bowl** LII596 $80
Cup and saucer U26 three for $180;
WS set of six $225; Rd set of six $390
10″ **plate** LII702 abt prf $65; WS $87.50; WS $80
8½″ **plate** WS two for $90
8¼″ **plate** U25 two for $140
8″ **plate** Rd $45
7½″ **plate** LII689 three for $110; WS two disc $50
7¼″ **plate** U25 and U29 three for $150
7″ **plate** Rd two for $88

811   Urn
a.   Sectional border
b.   Solid border

811a   Urn-sectional border
Cup and saucer-round Ho rpd $50; U22 $65; U22 crk $30; WS set of four $160; St25 four, some scaled and 8″ plate crk $150; Rd set of four $260

Cup and saucer-ridge side WS $40; WS chp $15
Coffee pot Ho rpd $140; Rd 11½″ $575
4¼″ **cup plate** Rd crk $130
10″ **plate** LII612 rim chp and wrn $20; LII688 disc $80; U22 $160
8¼″ **plate** LII611 two for $140; U22 $110; WS $50; Rd $75; Rd $45; Rd rpd $25
8¼″ **soup plate** He $45
7½″ **plate** U29 $110
7″ **plate** He25, 26 $100; He $42.50
6″ **plate** WS crk and disc $30
811b   Urn-solid border
7¼″ **plate** LII687 $60; WS $40

GAUDY DUTCH

812   War Bonnet
   6" bowl Rd $150
   4¾" cup plate LII686 $90; Rd crk $70
   4¼" cup plate LII685 $130
   Cup and saucer-straight side U21 $60; WS two for $90
   Cup and saucer-round LII585 two for $65
   10" plate He36, 37 two for $130
   10" soup plate U21 (Y746) three for $315; Rd two for $320
   9" plate Rd disc $72.50
   9" soup plate Rd $120
   8½" soup plate WS two for $65; WS wrn $27.50
   8" plate U20 five for $375; WS five for $337.50; WS wrn $27.50
   7" plate He24 rim chp $25
   7" soup plate U21 $65; Rd $80
   6" plate LII589 $70
   5" plate Rd crk $80
   LII587 5¼" plate prf and 4⅝" plate scaled on back $80

813   Strawflower (impressed RILEY)
   10" plate U22 $250
   8½" plate Rd $65

814   Zinnia (impressed RILEY)
   10" plate Rd $75
   10" soup plate LII704 $140

   9" plate Rd $80
   8⅜" plate LII692 $70; LII693 two almost prf $100
   8" plate St19 with 8¼" Dahlia $70

815   Leaf
   6" plate Rd $65

LII710 Single Rose small plate, Urn and Dahlia cups and Carnation cup and saucer-defects $45; LII711 Oyster cup and saucer prf, two Butterfly saucers, Oyster, Grape and Double Rose plates and an Oyster plate with b'ue transfer border. Some defects $50

War Bonnet	Single Rose	Strawflower	Carnation
Urn	Grape		Primrose
Carnation	Single Rose		Carnation

CYBIS MODERN ADAPTIONS

Boleslaw Cybis, a Polish artist known throughout the world, was commisioned by his government to paint two al fresco murals to appear at the 1939 New York World's Fair in the Polish Pavilion. About to return home, news arrived that the Nazis had invaded Poland. He turned around immediately and headed for the United States where he became an American citizen and remained until his death.

He turned to sculpture, his first love, for a livelihood, and opened a studio in Trenton, New Jersey where he developed his ceramic art. Gift shop hand-painted plaster of Paris figures were made first, and in 1942, he founded the Cordey China Company. He also produced coffee sets, decorated lamps, ceramic flowers, ribbons, porcelain lace, gift shop figurines, and wall plaques. These were manufactured by skilled and artistically talented Poles like himself. The items marked "Cordey" were made from 1942 to 1950. They are within the price range of the average collector.

After World War II, gift shops were flooded with imports from Europe and Japan, and Cordey production ceased. For the remainder of his life Mr. Cybis devoted his time and artistry to outstanding porcelains, perhaps, the highest form of ceramic art in this country. These hand-shaped porcelains, marked "Cybis," included exquisite work, much of it in limited editions which have been exhausted and are collected and displayed with pride. The editions included small and large florals, animals, Madonnas, children's heads, figures, and birds.

Although not antiques, many go to private and museum collections. United States presidents have faithfully chosen Cybis porcelains as gifts to heads of other nations.

The *Flower Bouquet of the United States* may be seen at the Smithsonian Institution, Washington, D.C., as each state flower is represented. It made its first appearance at the 1964-1965 World's Fair in New York. *The Holy Child of Prague* is in Washington at the National Shrine of the Immaculate Conception, where it has its own specially designed niche.

Sometime amid all the notoriety, Cybis got the idea to mass produce modern adaptions of Gaudy Dutch in the Butterfly pattern. The shapes included the Butterfly only, Butterfly between two sprays, in a cup plate, toddy plate, round cup and saucer, and experimental large plates.

The hard opaque porcelain paste was coated with a hard vitreous glaze which made the Gaudy Dutch show up brilliantly. The soft paste originals have quite a soft glaze from time and wear.

The first examples manufactured with a thin glaze were unmarked. When better examples were produced they were marked with a fine straight line "CYBIS." Apparently the marking die was too fine and soon broke, and a heavier model was used but that also failed. By this time the experimental costs were being considered and marking as a hand operation often resulted in broken blanks. These reasons plus high labor costs and objections from antique collectors caused the Gaudy Dutch venture to fail.

These experimental shapes were not intended to fool anyone and required quality workmanship and materials. The Gaudy Dutch Butterfly pieces that were released for market consumption were done by an elderly decorator who had learned his trade in Dresden. Today these pieces are collector's items!

GAUDY WELSH

Includes a study of the ware, patterns, colors, manufacturers, terminology, and prices.

FOREWORD

Part Two of this text reveals the great variety of shapes and patterns that are available for the collector to enjoy in Gaudy Welsh. Colored photographs of numerous shapes, plus descriptions of 125 designs will assist the viewer and reader in identifying objects when they are seen. The colored intensity of the patterns shown will enable one to understand the decorative motifs. Examples are described fully giving their heights/diameters, present values, and names when known. The history of various manufacturers is clarified along with marks that were used on Gaudy Welsh.

A comparison is made between colors and similarities and differences found in Gaudy Dutch and Gaudy Welsh designs. Described and evaluated are the uses of yellow, green, russet, pink, orange, and cobalt blue.

Discussed are the history of the potter's wheel and its evolution. A line drawing of an early Staffordshire potter's wheel is shown.

"The Potteries" in Stoke-on-Trent are focused upon for the tremendous impact they had on the china industry in England. The processes used to manufacturer china, dangers involved in the work, plus a discussion of the workers is covered.

A kiln's anatomy is described fully and a sketch shown, along with the heating process, updrafts, and the average firing times from beginning to end are volunteered.

Individual Gaudy Welsh shapes are identified. There is information concerning each and the era when fabrication took place.

Facts about earthenware, stoneware, and porcelain are included with basic ingredients used, characteristics of each ware, and its firing temperature. Hard and soft paste are distinguished from each other, their ingredients are elaborated upon, and firing temperatures are also included.

A chemical analysis of a variety of clays used is broken down by percentages, and the plasticity of numerous types of clay is related.

Population figures between 1801 and 1931 are presented for the British Isles, and then broken down into the countries of England, Wales, Scotland, and Ireland, respectively.

Immigrants coming to the United States are given as percentages beginning in 1820. A Pennsylvania map showing the counties enables the viewer to see the locales where Germans and Welsh settled. William Penn's contribution is noted so that a variety of sects could gain their freedom. Religious congregations in the United States in 1775-1776 are tallied. The reader will view a portion of Penn's pamphlets dealing with his acquisition, and population efforts to have this vast tract of land inhabited. The term Redemptioners is explained along with their difficult voyages across the Atlantic, their testimonies are given, the types of ships and their names are listed, plus the principal ports of embarkation are also covered.

Museum collections of Gaudy Dutch and Gaudy Welsh in the United States are listed. The names and locations of numerous European museums are also given. Sources where you may view, purchase, and have restoration work done, if necessary, are provided.

Additional ways of recognizing Gaudy Welsh are itemized, pottery and porcelain publications and their addresses are furnished, a complete glossary identifies needed terminology, a comprehensive guide gives prices, and an extensive bibliography rounds out the text. I believe that this portion of the book will give you a broad and complete understanding of Gaudy Welsh peasant luster.

INTRODUCTION
A Gaudy Ware Comparison

Gaudy Dutch and Gaudy Welsh possess a loosely knit kinship in that they both were manufactured in the British Isles, exported to the United States for a poor class of people, and have incorporated in their designs similar uses of colors and in some cases exhibit many complementary motifs. Gaudy Dutch was manufactured as a soft paste china from about 1790 to 1825 in 16 patterns, while Gaudy Welsh was fabricated from about 1820 to 1860 in perhaps as many as 300 patterns.

Much of the fine and expensive china of the 18th century was quite elegant and owned by the wealthy. Names like Crown Derby, Royal Worcester, Coalport, Chelsea, Caughley, Swansea, Spode, Ridgeway, Minton, and Leeds graced the tables of the well-to-do. Before too long English factories were turning out similar products, but of a lesser quality, so that the common gentry could also acquire and enjoy.

Quality porcelain was expensive because of the meticulous craftsmanship and time-consuming efforts that went into making the biscuit ware and decorating it with fine coloring and real gold. The process was hastened for the masses, thus "gaudy wares" came on the market.

Substitutions were used for the porcelain body to include earthenware, creamware, ironstone, and bone china. Using lusters instead of gold, and simplifying the decorative treatment resulted in sometimes successful imitations of finer wares.

Lacking acceptance in their country of origin, the Gaudies were exported to Pennsylvania where Gaudy Dutch caught on with that sect, as Gaudy Welsh seemed to appeal to the Welsh faction. Today both of these products are scattered widely throughout the states and avidly sought.

In appearance and quality Gaudy Dutch exists and is collected for its consistency and artistic renderings. Gaudy Welsh, on the other hand, displays a fair consistency in the use of colors, composition, and proportions, however, some is also clumsy, heavy, and poorly balanced, with patterns out of proportion, and the blue being runny and smudged.

Both Gaudy Dutch and Gaudy Welsh are seldom seen marked although over the years some examples of each have been discovered labeled. Gaudy Dutch when marked is usually identified as being made by Riley, Rogers, Davenport, or Wood. Cups and saucers in Gaudy Welsh may be labeled with a pattern number, some few examples carry their manufacturer's mark. After the American revolution and during the incidence of the War of 1812, it seems understandable that English manufacturers were very reticent to mark much of their exports wares as having been made in England.

Both types of china may be discovered in many assorted shapes. Some individuals collect only one form, such as teapots, mugs, cups and saucers, plates, creamers, pitchers, sugar bowls, and the like. Other individuals collect all the forms and patterns. As a rule, large hollow ware examples seem to be at a premium and much more difficult to incorporate into an extensive collection. Condition and price also come into play, as some individuals have the means to seek out and purchase the more advanced patterns and shapes.

In the uses of coloration Gaudy Dutch and Gaudy Welsh have both similarities and differences. Yellow was used sparingly or not at all on Gaudy Welsh patterns shading from a light to a lemon yellow hue. This color is found on Leek, Llanrug, Tulip, Anglesey, and Chintz designs. Yellow was used a great deal in Gaudy Dutch motifs for decorative borders on blue, veins on cobalt leaves, and shading of leaves or half of a leaf, flower centers, and the outlines of leaves.

Gaudy Welsh greens cover the color spectrum from a pale yellow green to a dark green. It was incorporated in border designs and in the execution of numerous leaf shapes. Gaudy Dutch greens shade from light to yellow green to dark green. A leaf may be entirely green, half green and half yellow, or a green and blue combination.

Russet or burnt orange on Gaudy Welsh ranges from a vibrant hue to a very subtle shading. This color was used widely on both large and small flowers in many shapes. Incorporated with blue, where the white color of the object is permitted to show in some patterns reveals a very attractive contrast. On Gaudy Dutch patterns, decorators chose to use burnt orange in many shades for assorted flower shapes and butterflies predominately; deep red and orange were employed for borders and floral buds, and a lighter pinkish orange was used to create a ground color on the Urn, Oyster, Grape, and Dove patterns, while shaded fence type panels are found on the Strawflower, Single Rose, and Double Rose patterns.

Cobalt blue as an underglazed color was incorporated on wide surface areas of Gaudy Welsh borders, as leaves, panels, vines and stems, for motifs, and as scrolling. Dark blue similar to that used on stoneware crocks is often enhanced with luster designs that appear on top of the blue. Pink and gold lusters may appear bright and garish on some examples, and subtle, subdued, or worn on others. Blue may also be discovered to be watery, dark, runny, or even absorbed into the backs of plates and other objects. Cobalt blue was used on Gaudy Dutch to create leaves, borders and their divisions, for outlining and veining, and as mound shapes on Butterfly, Carnation, Double Rose, Primrose, Single Rose, Strawflower, Sunflower, Zinnia, and No Name designs. A lighter blue was used internally with mound forms, and outlines in blue plus yellow decoration are common on the Oyster pattern.

Pink was employed by Gaudy Welsh decorators on a limited basis with these patterns: Columbine, Panelled Daisy, Feather, Pink Rose, Daisy, and Billingsley Rose. A Gaudy Dutch pink is found aiding in the shading of leaves, and on the body of the butterfly in the pattern of the same name. In the Double Rose pattern, a six-petaled flower is seen shading from a pink to a purple. Four pink leaves, three in clusters of three, and one in a cluster of five outline narrow green leaves on the Leaf pattern. A pinwheel shaped 12-petaled pink flower, having a yellow center with dark veins is seen on the Zinnia pattern.

A true orange is seldom, if ever seen, on Gaudy Welsh. In Gaudy Dutch, orange is shown on the Zinnia pattern as two flowers, one star shaped with five-pointed petals, and the other having 12 petals with a yellow center.

In both instances, the patterns reflect an oriental influence that the manufacturing firms decided to use on their wares. Each pattern in Gaudy Dutch and Gaudy Welsh holds a certain hypnotic trance over the real connoisseur and collector. One will find himself returning to the patterns, much like one does when viewing designs that are woven in fine oriental rugs. The blending of colors and shapes enthrall the viewer so that he tries to memorize the patterns but finds that it is an almost impossible undertaking.

Whichever ware you decide to collect, if not both, you will discover that a collection of this kind is a sound investment, and one that will bring unlimited hours of enjoyment. In almost all of the patterns, with the exception of a few transfers in Gaudy Welsh, the lush patterns are drawn freehand and express the artistic merits of decorators from another era. Both Gaudy Dutch and Gaudy Welsh should be enjoyed for their historical implications and their collectible nature for many years to come.

THROWING ON THE POTTER'S WHEEL

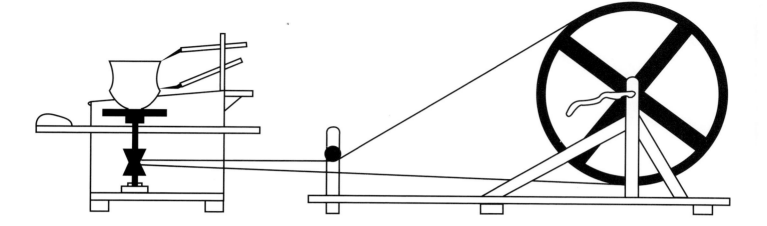

An early Staffordshire potter's wheel, driven by a rope pulley from a large flywheel turned by the thrower's assistant.

The potter's wheel dates back to the beginning of recorded history. This invention, a wheel spinning horizontally, transformed the manufacturing of large vessels, as it meant that they could be fabricated in a matter of minutes, whereas, the process might require several days. The craft of pot making was transformed from the hands of women as a result of mechanization into the hands of men. A specialization commenced, expert potters became traveling craftsmen, making and selling their pots where the demand was the greatest.

Some sources claim that the Chinese invented the potter's wheel, however, it appears more likely that the invention came from an area of the Fertile Crescent. Pottery found at Ur may be 5,000 years old and made on a wheel. The potter's wheel was also used in Assyria in the Chalcolithic Age, in Siyalk III in Iran, and in the Indus Valley Civilization in India by 2500 B.C.

Egypt may have been the place of origin for the potter's wheel. The turntable shaft was lengthened here about 3000 B.C. and a flywheel was added. The operation consisted of kicking the flywheel and later was moved by pulling the edge with the left hand while forming the clay with the right hand. Thus the anti-clockwise movement for the potter's wheel was developed which is fairly universal. Japan and parts of India use the clockwise motion.

Some potter's wheels consisted of a shaft having a throwing head on top and a heavy wheel that the potter turned with his feet until the proper speed was achieved. Double wheels were known, which were spun by an assistant, driven by a rope pulley.

Biblical potters' wheels probably were constructed of wood and clay, with some portions being stone. With a heavier flywheel, the wheel would turn longer once it was set in motion. References are made to ". . ." The potter's wheel . . ." in Jeremiah 18:3, and ". . . The potter sitting at his work . . ." in Ecclesiasticus 38:29.

IN AN EARLIER ERA

"The Potteries" consisting of six towns, each with its own town hall has become an enduring dynasty as a result of the men, women, and children who worked there in an earlier era. They were pioneers in the field of china and the memorials that they have left behind remain bright and extraordinary in this field of collecting.

Stoke-on-Trent probably became the china capitol of England because of all the raw materials that were present. There was lead and salt for glazing, an excess of coal to heat the kilns, and a variety of clays to be used in the manufacture of numerous types of china.

Youngsters either worked in the pottery factories or in the coal mines. Children who chose to work in the potteries put in a 12-hour day. Many perils befell them from lung disease created by the variety of factory fumes to the acrid smoke that poured from the bottle-shaped kilns, to the lead used in glazing and the poisonous arsenic used for painting which often resulted in potter's rot. Adults also contracted a great array of diseases and were not immune to their debilitation.

The potteries crushed clay through a process known as blunging, where the clay was mixed with water and stirred laboriously by hand with huge paddles to form slip. Traditionally pots were formed by throwing, as the clay was shaped by hand on the potter's wheel. Potters also cast their wares in plaster of Paris molds, a technique that was widely followed, and is in use even today. In this process the worker pours the slip into a moisture absorbent mold and pours out the excess. As the clay form dries, it shrinks, and then the object can be removed.

Jollying aided in creating bowls, cups, and tureens through the use of this machine. This forming tool descended into the clay inside a rotating mold, exerting pressure as the clay was forced against the mold.

Plates were formed from a wet ball of clay that was flattened into a "bat" or pancake and then placed on a horizontal, rotating plaster mold that shaped the inside of the form. A horizontal jig with the reverse mold for the back of the plate was then lowered onto the bat to create the opposite side.

During the past centuries, dried clay objects were placed in saggers (refractory containers). As many as 2,000 objects, stacked one on top of another, were placed in each bottle kiln. Then the doorway was bricked up, with just a peephole remaining so that the man in charge of firing the clay could control the results. The temperature was judged by the color of the flame, and the worker was often forced to remain at his station for 72 hours. During this crucial first firing, the temperature reached about 1,200 degrees Celsius. Workers were required to remove the saggers while the ovens were still hot, to get the maximum use out of the kilns after firing. Many kiln workers feared for their jobs, suffered from dehydration, or had their eyelashes, eyebrows, and mustaches singed from the heat.

The ware after the first firing is known as biscuit and can either be decorated under or over the glaze. With the application of the underglaze decoration, the biscuit is returned to the kiln for a second firing, at around 800 degrees Celsius to harden the color and rid the objects of oil. The ware is then dipped into a glaze, an opaque creamy liquid, which appears at completion as a sort of liquid glass. This result is produced when clay and flint are ground very fine, mixed with water, and fired. At this point the ware is fired for around 30 hours. The next firing at a reduced temperature permits more brilliant and assorted colors to be applied over the glaze. The number and the nature of the colors will determine how many additional firings at different temperatures will be required. It was often very tricky to achieve the desired colors. Red may have required orange paint with a pink over the top. Red directly applied would emerge from the kiln as a dirty gray. Lusters often lacked the proper brilliance or ended up being speckled, while cobalt blue had the property of running or bleeding through to the other side.

THE ANATOMY OF A KILN

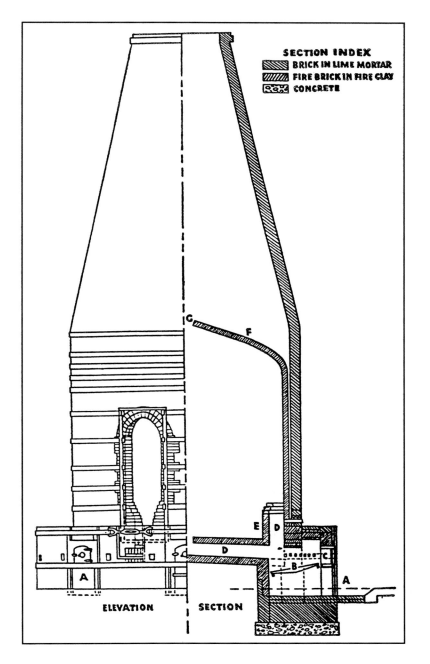

Pictured is a cross section of a bottle kiln similar to those used in the Staffordshire district. This large updraft kiln externally resembles a huge milk bottle having a broad sturdy base, and a short, stout neck. The fire-boxes are spaced within and around the base (A), usually eight in number, accompanying grates (B and C) were carefully adjusted to accommodate the coal. Above is the kiln's floor, pierced (D) to permit the maximum penetration of heat throughout the charge. Around the inside wall is a low secondary wall known as the bag-wall (E). Between it and the kiln's wall are the openings (D) that lead to the fire-box. The bag-wall's height is determined by the maximum heat striking the curved walls of the kiln. The dome (F) has a curved crown that throws back the waves of heat, reducing the minimum amount that escapes through the crown opening (G). The milk bottle stack aids in restraining the heat, and keeping outside air from hitting the crown. The stack's height increases the draft's effectiveness, similar to an extra few feet on a chimney which assists in making the furnace draw. The walls of the stack may also continue to the base of the kiln, forming an outer wall, with the fire-boxes placed within. In these kilns the men, while firing, stand inside the wall of the stack. This was a very hot and uncomfortable job.

RILEY

John and Richard Riley, Burslem (1802-1826). As brothers and partners, their Hill Works had a lucrative business. They are best known for their Gaudy Dutch derived from Imari patterns. When both brothers died in the same year, the firm assumed the name S. Alcock & Co.

Marks: (1) impressed RILEY, (2) impressed arc lettered RILEY, (3) printed floral spray background superimposed ribbon lettered RILEY, (4) printed oval buckled garter lettered RILEY'S above, centered Semi China.

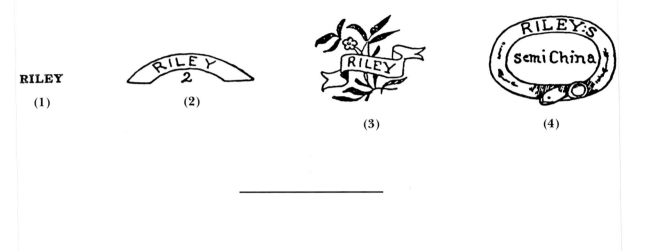

RILEY

(1)

(2)

(3)

(4)

ROGERS

Brothers John and George Rogers were partners at Longport and Burslem, (1786-1842). At the demise of George in 1815, the firm became known as John Rogers & Son. Spenser Rogers continued to use the same name after his father's death in 1816. The business was sold in 1842.

Marks: (1) impressed ROGERS, (2) impressed arrow symbol for iron with the word ROGERS below, (3) impressed JR/L, (4) impressed ROGERS & SON, (5) impressed J R S.

This firm also produced Gaudy Dutch.

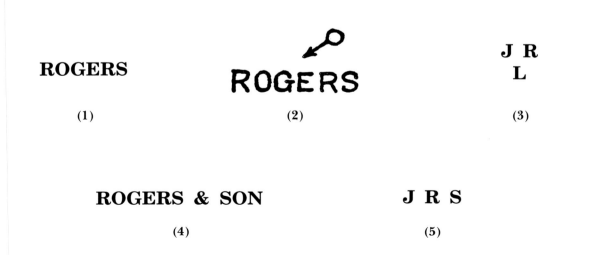

ROGERS

(1)

ROGERS

(2)

J R
L

(3)

ROGERS & SON

(4)

J R S

(5)

WOOD

Enoch Wood, Burslem, (1748-1840), was the son of Aaron Wood, a block cutter and modeler. Enoch the most versatile family member was born in 1759. His uncle living in Liverpool instructed him in art. An apprenticeship in pottery was accomplished under Humphrey Palmer of Hanley (1760-1776). He worked as a journeyman for just a short time and then he and his cousin, Ralph Wood purchased the Fountain Place pottery.

The partnership ended before 1790, and Enoch's next partner was James Caldwell. The firm became Wood & Caldwell lasting until 1818 when Enoch bought out Caldwell, a financial backer. His four sons, Thomas, Enoch, Edward, and Joseph, all trained potters, joined the firm which became Enoch Wood & Sons. After Enoch died in 1840, the sons continued the business until 1846. At that time the firm suspended work because of finances and was sold to Pinder, Bourne, and Hope. Wood also manufactured Gaudy Dutch.

The Fountain Place pottery during its 60 years of operation was expanded to occupy five older works and two branches for a limited time. Some experimental porcelain was made.

Marks: (1) impressed E WOOD, (2) impressed or incised on medallions ENOCH WOOD/SCULPSIT, (3) impressed or printed (1790), Enoch Wood & Co., (4) impressed (1790-1818), WOOD & CALDWELL, (5) printed and impressed, center spread eagle medallion, E WOOD & SONS in an arc above, SEMI CHINA below in an arc, WARRANTED below the eagle in an arc, (1818-1846), (6) arched cartouche with a spread eagle in the center, ENOCH WOOD & SONS in an arc above, BURSLEM is below, printed and sometimes without the framework, (7) printed floral sprays framing HARVARD COLLEGE and below E W & S and CELTIC CHINA, (8) impressed ENOCH WOOD & SONS/BURSLEM STAFFORDSHIRE, (9) impressed on porcelain, W (***), (10) ENOCH WOOD & SONS BURSLEM STAFFORDSHIRE, (11) very similar to number (6) without the arc and cartouche.

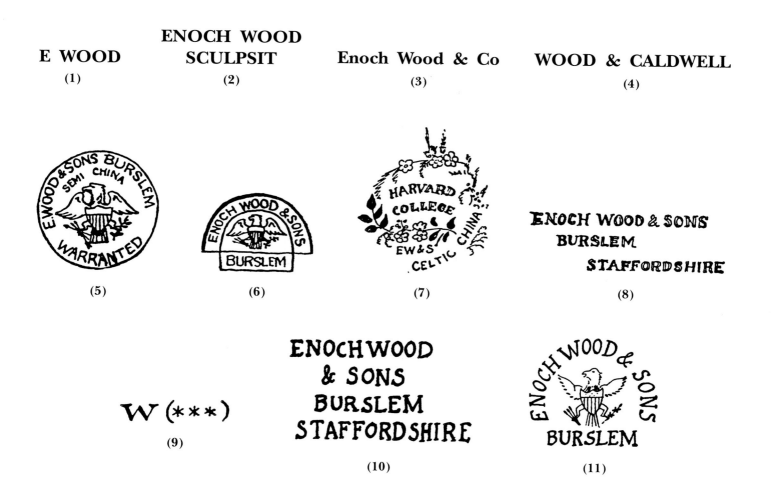

E WOOD
(1)

ENOCH WOOD
SCULPSIT
(2)

Enoch Wood & Co
(3)

WOOD & CALDWELL
(4)

(5)

(6)

(7)

ENOCH WOOD & SONS
BURSLEM
STAFFORDSHIRE
(8)

W (***)
(9)

ENOCH WOOD
& SONS
BURSLEM
STAFFORDSHIRE
(10)

(11)

ALLERTON

Charles Allerton and Sons were established in Longton, England in 1831 making Toby jugs, teapots, creamers, jugs in "peasant" floral designs, foliate patterns similar to Victorian Wedgwood Queensware, and a ware quite like Gaudy Welsh. The wares manufactured before 1870 were not marked. In 1890 Allerton began making jugs in the Oyster pattern. These wares are a heavier opaque porcelain and are usually stamped. Several other firms in Staffordshire reproduced Gaudy Welsh in the 20th century. The orange-red hues on these examples are often streaked and uneven. The firm went out of business in 1942.

Marks: (1) printed crown with ALLERTONS above in an arc, and ENGLAND is a straight line below, (2) two lines with CHA S ALLERTON & SONS above and ENGLAND centered below.

(1)

**CHA S ALLERTON & SONS
ENGLAND**

(2)

MALING

William Maling, a landowner in Sunderland, established the earliest and most important pottery in North Hylton called the Hylton Pot Works. About 1817, the Maling sons and their successors went to the Newcastle area, the Hylton factory was then controlled by John Phillips, the manager, or his son. The Garrison or Sunderland Pottery, a very large concern was already owned by the family.

The North Hylton factory made pink luster pottery and a creamware speciality group of mugs announcing births and marriages.

The Ouseburn Bridge Pottery was constructed by the Malings when they moved from Sunderland. It operated for many years. The existing New Ford Pottery was built on Tyneside in 1853 making domestic and specialized industrial earthenware.

Marks: (1) MALING impressed in an arc, (2) J. or JOHN PHILLIPS, (3) HYLTON POTTERY, (4) M is found on occasion.

(1)

J. or JOHN PHILLIPS
(2)

HYLTON POTTERY
(3)

M
(4)

SHERIFF HILL and TYNE

The Sheriff Hill and Tyne Potteries were owned by George Patterson, later he acquired Ford as his partner. The short-lived firm ended around 1892. Examples were made with cottage decorations and the wares may be discovered marked with a variety of names.

Marks: (1) SHERIFF HILL POTTERY, (2) FORD & PATTERSON, (3) PATTERSON & CO., (4) TYNE POTTERY.

SWANSEA

Swansea - Glamorgan, Wales. 1764-1870 - pottery; 1814-1822 - porcelain. William Coles manufacturer of redware established the Cambrian Pottery. At his demise in 1779, he was succeeded by his three sons. John Coles and George Haynes as Coles & Haynes were operating the pottery by 1790. In 1802, Coles left the firm and Haynes transferred the lease and controlling shares of stock to William Dillwyn for his son, Lewis Dillwyn. The firm of Haynes & Dillwyn was formed, Haynes was the manager.

Timothy Bevington, a Staffordshire potter and his son, John, replaced Haynes in 1810. The firm was then known as Dillwyn & Co. The Bevingtons and associates leased the pottery in 1817, working as Bevington & Co. Lewis Dillwyn continued the operation in 1824 when the lease expired, making earthenwares. In 1831, he and his father, William, became partners. Control went to David Evans and Gleason, his associate. Later Evan's son, J.D. Evans operated the pottery until it closed.

Swansea Pottery: In addition to redware other products included milkmaid figures, cow-shaped cream pitchers, black basalt, opaque china, Queensware, and transfer-decorated earthenware.

Swansea Porcelain: Porcelain making began in 1814 when William Billingsley plus 11 modelers and decorators, formerly from the Nantgarw porcelain factory near Cardiff started production. Lewis A. Dillwyn helped in forming the firm, and Billingsley was placed in charge. Porcelain kilns were installed but the firm failed because nine-tenths of the wares were ruined during firing. Billingsley was replaced by Timothy Bevington and new mixtures were adopted that would fire better. These also proved unsatisfactory and porcelain making halted in 1824 at Swansea when the Bevington lease expired.

Swansea fabricated a soft white paste porcelain having a green translucent tinge and a clear velvet glaze. Known as "duck egg," this porcelain is highly sought. Later types were more opaque and had either a yellow hue and a thin dull glaze or a white body with a glass glaze.

Porcelains were made in dessert and dinner services, vases, and other decorator pieces. Decorations included birds, monochrome landscapes, and multicolored flowers. Other motifs were strawberries, roses, elaborate fruit designs, ribbons and scrolls in gilt and colors, and applied flowers in high relief done in biscuit.

Marks: (1) impressed and used before 1800, CAMBRIAN in hand-lettered capitals. (2) impressed DILLWYN/ SWANSEA (1802-1817), (3) impressed DILLWYN & CO. in an arc above a number (1802-1817), (4) printed floral spray around CUBA, or other pattern with DILLWYN & CO. below (1824-1850), (5) printed scrolled cartouche lettered IMPROVED/STONEWARE/DILLWYN & CO. (1824-1850), (6) printed rectangular cartouche lettered DILLWYN'S/ETRUSCAN/WARE (1824-1850), (7) printed EVANS & GLEASON in an arc above SWANSEA, rectangle lettered BEST GOODS above pattern name CUBA (1850-1861), (8) impressed BEVINGTON & CO/SWANSEA (1817-1824), (9) impressed or printed SWANSEA on porcelain (1814-1822), (10) impressed SWANSEA above a horizontal trident (1814-1822), (11) in red, SWANSEA (1814-1822), (12) stringed instrument with CAMBRIAN POTTERY below (about 1780), (13) in capitals HAYNES, DILLWYN & Cº/CAMBRIAN POTTERY/SWANSEA (before 1802), (14) G.H. & CO. (early mark before 1802), (15) red or impressed Swansea in script (1814-1824), (16) red or impressed SWANSEA above two crossed tridents (about 1830), (17) red or impressed trident about the word SWANSEA (about 1830), (18) in capitals DILLWYN & CO. (1824-1850), (19) OPAQUE CHINA above SWANSEA (1824-1850), (20) DILLWYN in an enclosed arc (1824-1850), (20) DILLWYN in an enclosed arc (1824-1850), (21) NANTGARW mark with or without "CW" (China Works) used by William Billingsley (1814-1819), a decorator from Nantgarw.

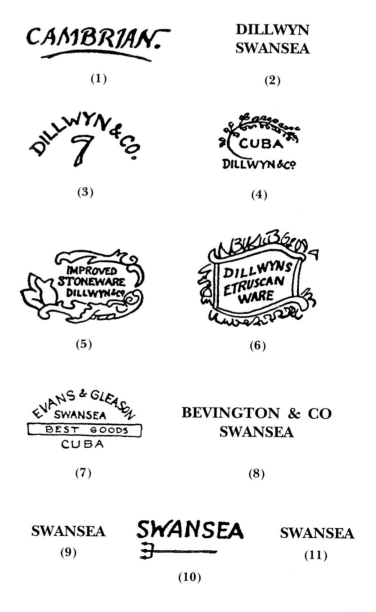

CAMBRIAN.

(1)

DILLWYN
SWANSEA

(2)

DILLWYN & CO.

(3)

CUBA
DILLWYN & CO.

(4)

IMPROVED
STONEWARE
DILLWYN & CO.

(5)

DILLWYNS
ETRUSCAN
WARE

(6)

EVANS & GLEASON
SWANSEA
BEST GOODS
CUBA

(7)

BEVINGTON & CO
SWANSEA

(8)

SWANSEA

(9)

SWANSEA

(10)

SWANSEA

(11)

SWANSEA - continued

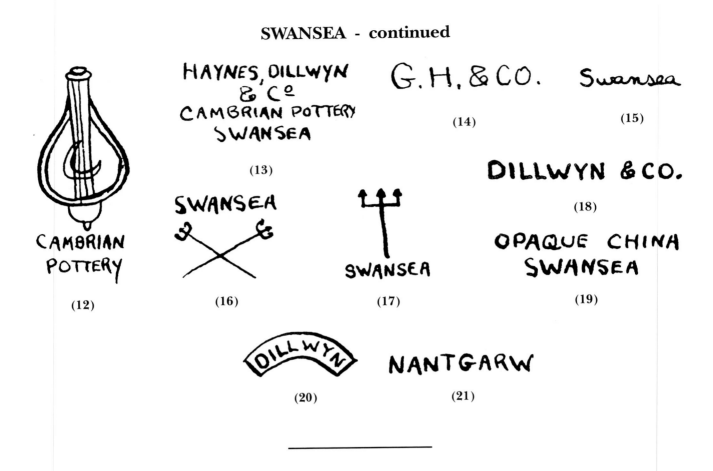

HAYNES, DILLWYN & C°
CAMBRIAN POTTERY
SWANSEA

(13)

CAMBRIAN POTTERY

(12)

SWANSEA

(16)

G.H. & CO.

(14)

Swansea

(15)

SWANSEA

(17)

DILLWYN & CO.

(18)

OPAQUE CHINA SWANSEA

(19)

DILLWYN

(20)

NANTGARW

(21)

DAWSON

One of the finest pottery firms on Wearside was founded by John Dawson and called Dawson's Pottery or Low Ford at South Hylton known then as Ford. Upon his death at age 88 in 1848, the firm was inherited by his grandson and deteriorated. When in full swing, the pottery manufactured novelties, marbles, high quality creamware, and earthenware tabletops with pictures of Napoleon's battles. Also produced were silver and copper luster and pink luster tea sets with cottage and primitive designs.

Marks: (1) impressed DAWSON (1800-1864), (2) impressed FORD (1800-1864), (3) impressed DAWSON & CO. in an arc with numbers and a rosette below (1800-1864), (4) impressed Ford Pottery, South Hylton in a straight line (1800-1864).

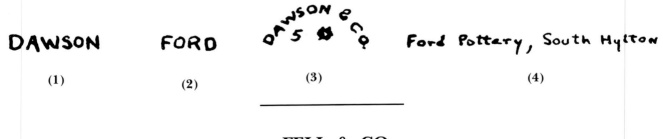

DAWSON

(1)

FORD

(2)

DAWSON & CO 5

(3)

Ford Pottery, South Hylton

(4)

FELL & CO.

Thomas Fell and Thomas Bell established the St. Peter's Pottery in 1817 which operated until 1890. They called their concern Thomas Fell & Co. The firm manufactured cream colored and white earthenware dishes and transfer wares decorated with willow and contemporary patterns.

Marks: (1) impressed FELL, (2) impressed T FELL & CO., sometimes with anchor and cable, (3) printed FELL/NEWCASTLE, (4) F & CO., (5) the single letter F.

MELLOR VENABLES

Mellor, Venables and Company operated in Burslem from 1818 to 1845. John Mellor operated a pottery near the market place. The Hole House Works was occupied by he and his partner, Venables in 1843.

Marks: (1) impressed MELLOR VENABLES & CO., (2) impressed in a circle, MELLOR VENABLES & CO., (3) printed urn with flowers and the words MELLOR VENABLES & C° below.

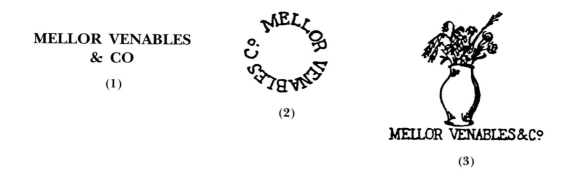

MELLOR VENABLES
& CO

(1)

(2)

MELLOR VENABLES&C°

(3)

PHILLIPS

The Sunderland or Garrison Pottery was established near a barracks at the east end of the town. The mark of Dixon and Austin sometimes includes the name Phillips. The firm was taken over by John Phillips of the North Hylton Pottery. From 1828, this establishment was known as Dixon, Austin & Co., the concern closed in 1865 and their transfer plates were purchased by the Ball Brothers and used in their Deptford (Sunderland) Pottery.

The company made Easter and birthday eggs, two-handled luster chamber pots, rolling pins, carpet balls, tea sets with the cottage pattern, religious plaques, copper and silver luster jugs noting the marriage of Queen Victoria in 1840, ornamental dogs with copper luster spots, greyhounds, and watch and clock stands.

Marks: (1) PHILLIPS & CO., (1800-1817), (2) Phillips & C°, Sunderland, 1813 (1800-1817), (3) J. PHILLIPS, HYLTON POTTERY (established 1780), (4) DIXON, AUSTIN, PHILLIPS & CO. (from 1817), (5) DIXON, PHILLIPS & CO., successors to Dixon, Austin, Phillips & Co., (6) W. DIXON, (7) DIXON & CO., (8) DIXON & CO., SUNDERLAND POTTERY, (9) DIXON, AUSTIN & CO., (10) DIXON & CO.

PHILLIPS & CO.

(1)

Phillips & C°, Sunderland, 1813

(2)

J. PHILLIPS, HYLTON POTTERY

(3)

DIXON, AUSTIN, PHILLIPS & CO.

(4)

DIXON, PHILLIPS & CO.

(5)

W. DIXON

(6)

DIXON & CO.

(7)

DIXON & CO., SUNDERLAND POTTERY

(8)

(9) DIXON, AUSTIN & CO.

DIXON & CO. (10)

JOHN MEIR

John Meir, an early producer of Gaudy Welsh, was working in 1812 in Tunstall. Meir also produced earthenware at Greengates Pottery which had been owned by William Adams. He had built the factory in 1834. The firm's name, John Meir, was changed to John Meir and Son in 1837. The Adams family also produced Gaudy Welsh in the butterfly pattern impressed with an eagle.
Marks: (1) JOHN MEIR, (2) JOHN MEIR & SON.

SOUTH WALES POTTERY

West of Swansea, the South Wales Pottery at Llanelly began operating in 1840 under the direction of William Chambers, Junior. The firm exported wares to the United States including Gaudy Welsh, porcelain, white granite, transfer and hand painted goods for the U.S. market from the 1850s. Some examples are found impressed SOUTH WALES POTTERY.
Mark: (1) impressed SOUTH WALES POTTERY.

WALLEY

In 1831, Elijah Jones commenced operating the Villa Pottery at Cobridge. Jones took on as his partner Edward Walley in 1841, and the firm went under the name Jones and Walley. Walley operated the business by himself from 1845 to 1856. Gaudy Welsh decors on ironstone, parian, and earthenwares were manufactured. The decorated ironstone found a ready market in the Pennsylvania Dutch area. It is possible that they also produced true Gaudy Welsh.

Marks: (1) impressed circle with WALLEY centered and IRONSTONE CHINA around the edge, (2) a coat of arms with a lion and unicorn with the words EDWARD WALLEY/COBRIDGE/STAFFORDSHIRE beneath, (3) impressed circle having the English registry mark centered and E. WALLEY NIAGARA SHAPE around the edge, (4) printed cartouche with the pattern name centered and E. WALLEY underneath.

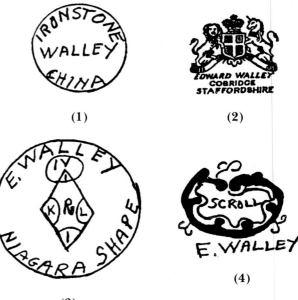

(1)   (2)

(3)

(4)

(*) *Authenticates firms as Gaudy Welsh producers.*

* Cambrian Pottery, Swansea, DILLWYN SWANSEA
* South Wales Pottery, Llanelly
* Glamorgan Pottery, Swansea, Wales
* MALING - Hylton Pottery and Ford Pottery
* Saint Peter's Pottery, Newcastle-on-Tyne, Northumberland, FELL & CO.
* Sheriff Hill Pottery
* Richard Davies and Company, Salt Meadows, South Shore, Gateshead
* Garrison Pottery, Sunderland (Dixon & Company)
* Dawson's Pottery, South Hylton

* John Meir, Tunstall
* The Adams family - Impressed eagle with wings spread, head facing to the left, left talon holding a branch and right talon holding three arrows.
* Enoch Wood, Burslem
* Wedgwood
  John Davenport, Longport - ?
  Mellor, Venables and Company, Burslem - ?
  Thomas Walker, Tunstall - ?
  Spode - ?
  Bayley and Ball, Longton - ?
  Ralph Stevenson - ?

Ridgway - ?
Minton - ?
Copeland and Garrett - ?
Bailey and Batkin - ?

Charles Allerton and Sons, Park Works; Longton, James Kent, Old Castle and Lingard all manufactured reproductions of the Oyster pattern. Also copied by Allerton were the Wagon Wheel pattern jugs of Edward Walley.

MAJOR GAUDY WELSH SHAPES

1. Jugs - Manufactured in earthenware and porcelain during the 1830's and 1840's. Used for decorative purposes and originally displayed on Welsh dressers.

2. Mugs - Fabricated of earthenware in numerous styles and sizes. Common children's mugs possess strap handles. Large mugs from the 1840-1850's made of porcelain have both ornate handles and involved body forms.

3. Tea Sets - Made of porcelain in Staffordshire after 1820. Most sets have pattern numbers. Sets consisted of a sugar bowl and creamer, teapot, two serving plates, a "slop" bowl, and six to 12 cups and saucers.

4. Plates - Came in many sizes, shapes and interesting patterns.

5. Miniatures - Found as children's tea sets, tobies, salt dishes, basins and ewers, and other related items.

6. Oddities - Vases, lidded quill holders, etc.

DATING GAUDY WELSH SHAPES

JUGS	1820-1840	Bulbous, high-waisted, curved spouts, ear-shaped handles, also octagonal sided, handles level with tops.
	1830-1845	Large lipped, lower waisted, flared and fluted rims, ornate thorn handles raised above top lip.
	1845-1860	Elongated bodies, short lips, high waisted, unusual shaped handles with gap between it and the body along the rim.
CUPS	1820-1840	Tall and concave or eight-sided shapes, some handleless to simple twig, ring, or loop handles.
	1830-1845	Lower waisted, flared drinking rims, pedestal bases, ornate handles attached below the top edge.
	1845-1860	Squat shorter bodies, handles often raised above the top lip and not so exaggerated, smaller bases.
TEAPOTS CREAMERS SUGARS	1830-1840	Extremely large, cumbersome to handle, goose-necked spouts, button and pointed finials.
	1840-1850	Size reduced, ornamented loop and elaborate pedestals, shorter spouts, some have ring finials.
	1850-1860	Overall sizes and decoration well under control and refined.

FACTS CONCERNING CHINA

All kinds of glazed earthenware and porcelain come under the classification of china. Since the beginning of the 17th century the word has been part of our language. Originally it was a Persian word, sounded phonetically as CHINI, meaning wares that reached a country from the lands of Manchu and Ming emperors by caravan.

The three major kinds of china are earthenware, stoneware, and porcelain. Earthenware includes wares made from available clays that are opaque when held to the light. Content varies considerably from the crudest folk pottery made from bank clay to other types which are more refined. Stoneware fired at high temperatures, around 2,400 degrees Fahrenheit, becomes vitrified and acquires a density and hardness similar to stone. The term porcelain designates the finest grade and most expensive china. When held to the light it varies in its degrees of translucency. The name is Portuguese in origin and "Porcellana" was the name used for the fine wares which the Portugese brought back from the colony of Macao, the first European trading settlement on the China coast.

All three - earthenware, stoneware, and porcelain - required one basic ingredient which is a select clay carefully mixed with other minerals. True Chinese porcelain, for example, was fabricated from a mixture of about 65 percent white kaolin and 35 percent powdered stone, called "petuntse" by the Chinese. The mixture at the Ching-te-Chen potteries varied according to the quality of porcelain to be fired.

Wedgwood evolved Queensware by improving ordinary Staffordshire cream-colored ware, by mixing white Devonshire with Dorsetshire clays and then adding a proportion of powdered calcinated flint. With the discovery of china clay deposits in Cornwell around 1770, he improved his Queensware by adding proportions of each. Mason's ironstone china, patented in 1813, comprised a mixture of Cornwall stone and clay, powdered iron slag, calcinated flint, and a small amount of oxide of cobalt. Josiah Spode II English bone china, perfected in 1800, was a result of mixing powdered cattle bones, kaolin, and feldspar in nearly equal portions. The cattle bone was also burned.

The word porcelain is derived from an Italian word "porcellana" meaning cowry-shell. Porcelain ware china is called by that name since it was first made by the Chinese. Porcelain made from purified clay and then baked, produces a hard, translucent material; its thickness determines the transparency.

Paste, the body of which an article is manufactured, may be either hard or soft. Hard paste made of natural clay appears fine grained, sparkling, and vitreous when broken. Soft paste is dull and more porous, being fabricated from artifical clays.

The shiny material which covers the paste is called glaze. Hard glaze makes the object cold to the touch, it is also thin and colorless. Soft glaze may be scratched with a sharp object, it does not feel cold, and is gummy to the touch. The rims on which hard paste porcelain rest are not glazed. This is a very easy method of distinguishing hard from soft paste porcelain.

Hard glaze porcelain was made at Liverpool, Bristol, and Plymouth. Soft glaze was manufactured at Rockingham, Liverpool, Dow, Derby, Chelsea, and Worcester. Staffordshire porcelain was a soft glaze with feldspar added.

Biscuit is a term applied to pottery and porcelain before they are enameled or glazed. Being a dead white, biscuit ware requires glaze to bring out its beauty.

"Faience," a French word, applies to all types of glazed earthenware, not to include porcelain. Majolica, meaning the same thing as faience formerly dealt exclusively with Italian decorated pottery of the 15th through 18th centuries, made in the old Italian style.

Stoneware is seldom dipped, instead the glazing and firing are usually accomplished at the same time by throwing salt into the kiln.

Semi-china is made with a large mixture of feldspar and is almost as translucent as porcelain. Their main differences are due to the way they are prepared, to a few minor ingredients, and to the degrees of heat that they are subjected to.

On most every piece of old china, especially flat ware, you will discover three rough spots in the glaze, on the face, but more often on the back of each example. Being equidistant and in groups of three, these are termed stilt marks. The "stilts" or little tripods were placed between the pieces to separate them when they were being fired in the kiln. An example in proof condition will have no chips or cracks, have fine color or printing, and not be scratched or greased. Some examples may have crazes or show minimal signs of wear but otherwise be in perfect condition. Cracks detract more from the value than do chips and nicks. We say a piece is greased when much dirt has penetrated the glaze or spoiled the colors.

Pottery took rapid strides at the beginning of the 18th century. Between 1722 and 1749 at least nine patents were taken out. Early domestic examples included Bellarmines, copied from German ale jugs, stoneware, a variety of drinking vessels, mugs, and posset-pots.

The mug was derived from drinking cups generally decorated with a grotesque, rude face or "mug." Posset-pots were used for supper on Christmas eve. Into the tasty drink garnished with spices were dropped the wedding ring of the hostess and a piece of silver. Each guest had their turn at fishing - the one who retrieved the ring was guaranteed a speedy and happy marriage; the one who got the coin was certain to have good luck during the next year.

KINDS OF PORCELAIN

Hard-paste and soft-paste porcelain are distinguished according to the composition of the porcelain paste and the glaze. Bone china is a speciality type located halfway between the two.

Hard-paste porcelain consists of two ingredients: pure china (greasy, very plastic and difficult to fuse) combined with white mica (fairly easy to fuse). Quartz or sand may be added but the porcelain properties depend on the ratio of felspar and china clay. If the paste contains a great deal of china clay, it will fuse less easily but will be harder. A mixture is grounded, kneaded, washed, and then dried to yield a plastic dough that can be poured into molds or turned on a potter's wheel. After the pieces are shaped, they are fired twice at 600-800 degrees and then after glazing at 1,300-1,500 degrees Celsius. Since the glaze is the same substance as the body, although in different proportions, it will fuse with the body and cannot be scraped and will not flake. Hard-paste porcelain like its name is distinguished by hardness, resistance to heat and acids, impermeability, transparency, a shell-like appearance at a surface break, and its bell-like sound when tapped.

Soft-paste porcelain is known as artificial and frit porcelain. It consists of a mixture of vitreous substances, a frit containing sand or flint, saltpeter, sea salt, soda, alum, and alabaster. The mixture is permitted to fuse for a certain period of time and marl, containing clay and gypsum is then added. This fused, vitreous substance mixed with clay is ground and filtered until it is plastic. Modeled examples are fired at 1,100-1,500 degrees Celsius and allowed to dry and become porous. The glass glaze fuses easily and is rich in lead oxide and also contains lime, sand, soda, and potash. Glazed examples are fired a second time at 1,050-1,100 degrees Celsius to force the glaze to merge with the body. Soft-paste porcelain is more translucent than hard-paste and is a softer, almost creamy white color. It does not resist heat, and a break reveals a straight line. Its unglazed surface has a granular appearance.

Bone china, a compromise between hard-paste and soft-paste, was discovered in England and first made there about 1750. Its ingredients are china clay, feldspar and calcium phosphate from bone ash which makes it easier to fuse. Fired at 1,100-1,500 degrees Celsius, the result is a hard-paste porcelain softened with the addition of bone ash. Its glaze is basically the same as soft-paste porcelain, but also contains lead oxide and borax which makes it merge easier with the body. The glazes fuse at a certain temperature and joins to the body firmly. Bone china's peculiar properties place it halfway between hard-paste and soft-paste porcelain in quality. Bone china wears better, is harder, and less permeable than soft-paste porcelain, but has the same soft glaze. Whiter than soft-paste, it is less white than hard-paste porcelain.

Similar types of molds were used to create china. *The Penny Magazine*, **February 1843.**

CLAYS AND CHEMICAL ANALYSIS

Material	SiO_2	Al_2O_3	Fe_2O_3	TiO_2	CaO	MgO	K_2O	Na_2O	Li_2O	Ignition Loss
Red Dalton Clay	63.2	18.3	6.3	1.3	0.3	0.5	1.6	1.2		6.4
Barnard Clay	41.4	6.7	29.9	0.2	0.5	0.6	1.0	0.5		8.4
Monmouth Stoneware	56.8	28.5			0.3	0.3	0.3	1.3		12.2
Jordon Stoneware	69.4	17.7	1.6	1.3	0.1	0.5	1.5	1.39		6.4
Albany Slip	57.6	14.6	5.2	0.4	5.8	2.7	3.2	0.8		9.5
Ball Clay	51.9	31.7	0.8	1.5	0.2	0.2	0.9	0.4		12.3
Saggar Clay	59.4	27.2	0.7	1.6	0.6	0.2	0.7	0.3		9.4
Fireclay	58.1	23.1	2.4	1.4	0.8	1.1	1.9	0.3		10.5
Georgia Kaolin	44.9	38.9	0.4	1.3	0.1	0.1	0.2	0.2		14.21
English Kaolin	47.25	37.29	0.84	0.05	0.03	0.28	1.80	0.04		12.21
Kyanite	59.05	36.5	0.16	0.67	0.03	0.01		0.18		0.21
Pyrophyllite	73.5	20.0	0.5		0.1		1.4	1.2		3.3
Bentonite	64.32	20.7	3.47	0.11	0.46	2.26	2.9			5.15
Volcanic Ash	72.51	11.55	1.21	0.54	0.68	0.07	7.87	1.79		3.81
Plastic Vitrox	75.56	14.87	0.09		0.22	0.20	6.81	0.29		2.04
Feldspar/Potash	86.3	17.9	0.08		0.4		10.10	3.10		0.32
Cornwall Stone	72.6	16.1	0.23	0.06	1.4	0.1	4.56	3.67		2.54
Nepheline Syenite	60.4	23.6	0.08		0.7	0.1	9.8	4.6		0.7
Lepidolite	55.0	25.0	0.08				9.0	1.0	4.0	0.92x
Spodumene	62.91	28.42	.053		0.11	0.13	0.69	0.46	6.78	0.28

x - Add five percent Fluorine

SiO_2 - Flint (quartz, silica) TiO_2 - Titanium Dioxide K_2O - Formula for Nepheline Syenite
Al_2O_3 - Kaolin (calcined)   CaO - Formula for Cornwall Stone Na_2O - Formula for Cornwall Stone
Fe_2O_3 - Iron Oxide, Red (ferric)   MgO - Formula for Cornwall Stone Li_2O - Spodumene

PLASTICITY OF CLAY VARIETIES

Washed Kaolin	44.48 - 47.50	Flint Fire Clays	8.89 - 19.04
White Sedimentary Kaolin	28.60 - 56.25	Saggar Clays	18.40 - 28.56
Ball Clay	25.00 - 53.30	Stoneware Clays	19.16 - 34.80
Plastic Fire Clays	12.90 - 37.40	Brick Clays	13.20 - 40.70

$$\text{Water of Plasticity} = \frac{\text{weight of plastic sample - weight of dry sample}}{\text{weight of the dry sample}} \times 100$$

MANUFACTURING OF CHINA, POTTERY, AND EARTHENWARE

The census of 1921 indicates that 72% of all males in England and Wales were located in Staffordshire; the female proportion was 80% with 66% in the Stoke County Borough. Illustrated is the remarkable concentration of this industry in the North Staffordshire coalfield.

Throughout the world the North Staffordshire coalfield has become linked with the pottery industry and is known as "The Potteries." This region in northern Staffordshire, England was and still is the country's main producer of china and earthenware. The area extends nine miles from southeast to northwest, and three miles from northeast to southwest to include the former towns of Longton, Hanley, Burslem, Tunstall, and Stoke-upon-Trent. In 1910, the six were federated as the municipal borough of Stoke-on-Trent, which became a city in 1925. Josiah Wedgwood opened his pottery at Etruria in 1769, which is now called Barlaston. Coal from the north Staffordshire coalfield and coarse clay are the local products used in this industry.

The triangular shaped coalfield is situated in the southwest corner of the Pennines. A number of southward flowing streams unite forming the headwaters of the Trent. After a southward direction, it flows around the southern end of the Pennines and then moves northward. A low divide of 500 feet in height separates the headwaters of these streams from the Cheshire Plain. In the northeast are the Millstone Grit highlands of the Pennines. Thus, the North Staffordshire coalfield is curiously isolated by natural formations. It is difficult to explain the reason why the pottery industry should have become concentrated in this region. No records of any pottery works in this area exist before the 17th century. During the Middle Ages, rough earthenware pots were made throughout the countryside as a typical domestic industry. Coal replaced wood for firing in the 17th century, and in the coalfields, there were also belts of clay that were used for rough pottery making. Perhaps the industry was favored in the Staffordshire coalfields because of its isolation and the poverty of this region in agriculture. Pots were fabricated in a shed built near the dwelling house. Men dug their own clay, and some of the families also dug the coal which fired the ovens. Lead for powder glazing was mined from the Carboniferous Limestone of the Derbyshire Dome. Over the years, a large number of skilled master potters grew, inventing salt glazing and the use of molds. Soon greater care was given to selecting clays and noting their color and consistency. The industry was an important one by the middle of the 18th century, so much so that special clays were imported along with flints from Devon and Dorset. Additionally, heavy earthenware and firebricks were made. The district became noted for chinaware, after the importation of china clay from Cornwall, beginning in 1770. Also in 1770, after much construction difficulty, the Trent and Mersey Canal was opened. Before the canal, flint stones were brought by sea from the coast to Hull and Liverpool and then there was still the overland journey to the Potteries. The canal provided a direct water route between Cornwall and Staffordshire. All china clay from the southwest found its way to the Staffordshire coalfield. The Mersey-Trent Canal departed the Mersey near Runcorn and connected with the Bridgewater Canal, the forerunner of the Manchester Ship Canal. The canal passed through the western hill barrier of the Potteries by the Harecastle tunnel. In its course of 93 miles, there were 75 locks. From the Potteries, there was navigable water to Hull and so a connection was established between Liverpool, Hull, and the Potteries. The pottery towns spread themselves out in a line following the bands of clays utilized most. The chief centers, mentioned previously and including Fenton, had a population of nearly 300,000 in 1925. The tread continues even today, and there are over 300 pottery works along with a variety of connected industries, for example the manufacture of required machinery, stains, colors, glazes, chemicals, and brushes.

POPULATION TALLIES (1801-1931)

Date	British Isles	England and Wales	Scotland	Ireland
1801	- -	8,892,536	1,608,420	- -
1811	- -	10,164,256	1,805,864	- -
1821	20,893,584	12,000,236	2,091,521	6,801,827
1831	24,028,584	13,896,797	2,364,386	7,767,401
1841	26,730,929	15,914,148	2,620,184	8,196,597
1851	27,390,629	17,927,609	2,888,742	6,574,278
1861	28,927,485	20,066,224	3,062,294	5,798,967
1871	31,484,661	22,712,266	3,360,018	5,412,377
1881	34,884,848	25,974,439	3,735,573	5,174,836
1891	37,732,922	29,002,525	4,025,647	4,704,750
1901	41,458,721	32,527,843	4,472,103	4,458,775
1911	45,213,347	36,070,492	4,760,904	4,381,951
1921	- -	37,886,699	4,882,497	
				4,228,553*
1931	- -	39,946,931	4,842,554	

* The census year for the Irish Free State and Northern Ireland was 1926.

IMMIGRANTS TO THE UNITED STATES
BY NATION OF ORIGIN

Date	Great Britain	Ireland	Scandinavia	Other NW Europe (a)	Germany	Italy
1820-1829	20.5%	40.2%	0.2%	9.3%	4.5%	0.3%
1830-1839	13.8	31.7	0.4	8.4	23.2	0.4
1840-1849	15.3	46.0	0.9	6.4	27.0	0.1
1850-1859	15.8	36.6	0.9	4.4	34.7	0.3
1860-1869	25.6	20.5	4.6	3.4	43.7	0.5
1870-1879	21.1	15.4	7.6	4.3	27.4	1.7
1880-1889	15.4	12.8	12.8	3.8	27.6	5.1
1890-1899	8.9	11.0	10.6	3.3	15.7	16.3
1900-1909	5.7	4.3	5.9	2.2	4.0	23.5
1910-1919	5.8	2.6	3.8	2.5	2.8	19.4
1920-1929	7.9	4.8	4.7	3.2	9.0	12.3
1930-1939	7.7	5.1	2.4	4.6	17.1	12.2
1940-1949	14.6	2.6	2.6	8.7	13.9	5.9
1950-1959	12.4	2.4	2.1	6.3	24.6	8.0
1960-1969	7.1	1.3	1.4	3.7	6.5	6.2
Total in thousands	**4,889** **10.9%**	**4,714** **10.6%**	**2,473** **5.6%**	**1,635** **3.7%**	**6,896** **15.2%**	**5,149** **11.5%**

(a) Switzerland, Belgium, France, Netherland, Luxembourg

Date	Spain, Portugal, and Greece	Eastern Europe (b)	U.S.S.R. and Baltic States	Asia	Canada	Latin America (c)	All Other Countries
1820-1829	2.1%	- -	0.1%	- -	1.8%	5.8%	15.2%
1830-1839	0.5	0.1	- -	- -	2.2	3.7	15.6
1840-1849	0.1	- -	- -	- -	2.4	1.1	0.5
1850-1859	0.4	0.1	- -	1.3	2.3	0.7	2.7
1860-1869	0.4	0.2	0.1	2.6	5.7	0.6	0.9
1870-1879	0.7	2.6	1.3	4.9	11.8	0.8	0.4
1880-1889	0.4	6.9	3.5	1.3	9.4	0.6	0.3
1890-1899	1.3	17.7	12.2	1.6	0.1	0.9	0.4
1900-1909	2.9	26.3	18.3	2.9	1.5	1.9	0.6
1910-1919	5.7	19.9	17.4	3.1	11.2	5.7	0.3
1920-1929	3.8	12.1	2.1	2.6	22.1	14.9	0.4
1930-1939	3.3	10.0	1.3	2.6	23.3	9.5	0.8
1940-1949	2.4	3.9	0.5	3.5	18.8	19.5	2.9
1950-1959	2.8	5.6	0.1	5.7	15.3	12.6	1.8
1960-1969	6.0	3.6	0.1	11.0	13.5	38.9	1.1
Total in thousands	**1,155** **2.6%**	**5,384** **12.1%**	**3,387** **7.6%**	**1,431** **3.2%**	**3,942** **8.9%**	**3,087** **6.9%**	**463** **1.0%**

(b) Yugoslavia, Albania, Bulgaria, Austria, Hungary, Czechoslovakia, Rumania, Poland, Turkey
(c) Not included are persons born in Puerto Rico, the Virgin Islands, and the Canal Zone

Date	Total Number In Thousands
1820-1829	129
1830-1839	538
1840-1849	1,427
1850-1859	2,815
1860-1869	2,081
1870-1879	2,742
1880-1889	5,249
1890-1899	3,694
1900-1909	8,202
1910-1919	6,347
1920-1929	4,296
1930-1939	699
1940-1949	857
1950-1959	2,300
1960-1969	3,212

PENNSYLVANIA COUNTIES

1. Erie	23. Clarion	45. Perry
2. Warren	24. Jefferson	46. Dauphin
3. McKean	25. Clearfield	47. Lebanon
4. Potter	26. Center	48. Schuylkill
5. Tioga	27. Union	49. Berks
6. Bradford	28. Northumberland	50. Lehigh
7. Susquehanna	29. Montour	51. Northampton
8. Wayne	30. Columbia	52. Bucks
9. Crawford	31. Luzerne	53. Montgomery
10. Mercer	32. Monroe	54. Washington
11. Venango	33. Carbon	55. Fayette
12. Forest	34. Beaver	56. Greene
13. Elk	35. Allegheny	57. Somerset
14. Cameron	36. Armstrong	58. Bedford
15. Clinton	37. Westmoreland	59. Fulton
16. Lycoming	38. Indiana	60. Franklin
17. Sullivan	39. Cambria	61. Cumberland
18. Wyoming	40. Blair	62. Adams
19. Lackawanna	41. Huntingdon	63. York
20. Pike	42. Mifflin	64. Lancaster
21. Lawrence	43. Snyder	65. Chester
22. Butler	44. Juniata	66. Delaware
		67. Philadelphia

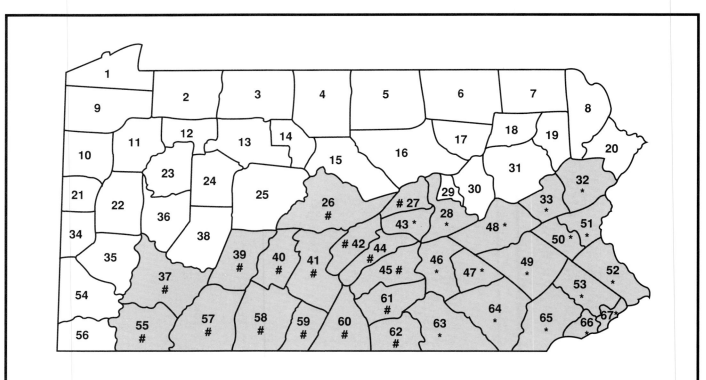

Pennsylvania County Map Showing The Distribution of Pennsylvania Germans

* Pennsylvania German Counties
 # Counties With Pennsylvania German Sections

A QUAKER COLONY IN AMERICA

In 1666, William Penn sought to establish a colony in America for Quakers who suffered under the persecution of the "Clarenden Code." After King Charles II granted Penn land for this purpose he wrote his *Frame of Government* for the Colony and sent commissioners to lay out a "great town" in a systematic fashion, which was named Philadelphia. With his faith in humanity, he gave the people more powers and privileges than the colonists possessed in any other Colony. Absolute religious freedom was the most important and the most remarkable concession. Those eligible to vote and hold offices were all Christians holding certain amounts of property. The death penalty in Penn's Colony was only carried out for treason and murder. Philadelphia was advantageously laid out facing both the Schuylkill and Delaware Rivers. Growth and prosperity began almost immediately. After Penn's arrival in the Colony in 1682, an assembly held at Upland adopted Penn's plan of government. Penn made his "Great Treaty" with the Indians in 1683. It was "the only treaty not sworn to and never broken," according to Voltaire.

The oppressed and persecuted from many lands came to this Colony for refuge. The Quaker faction was the dominant element until the Revolutionary War. Some Quakers of Welsh stock settled a large colony in the "Welsh barony" in Delaware and Montgomery Counties. Pastorious, a remarkable leader, brought vast numbers of Mennonites in 1682-1683 to settle Germantown. It became the leading German community in America and was the home of numerous early industries in Pennsylvania. Large colonies of Germans from the Palatine countries, members of the Reformed and Lutheran Churches settled on the fertile ground running from Easton, through Allentown, Reading and Lebanon to the Cumberland Valley. Important centers were founded by the Moravians at Bethlehem and Nazareth. The Scotch-Irish Presbyterians were an active and restless pioneer group that occupied the back country on the frontier. Different in temperament from the Quakers and Germans, the Scotch-Irish formed an element of opposition to the ruling groups all through the 18th century. Large colonies of Connecticut "Yankee" settled after 1770 in the Wyoming and Muncy Valleys.

The population of the state was 602,000 in 1800. Prior to and just after the Revolutionary War, settlements spread beyond the mountains. The Upper Susquehanna Valley was rapidly settled during this period. Bridges, roads, and stagecoach routes were established in every direction. The first important turnpike in America was the Philadelphia-Lancaster turnpike completed in 1790. A bill passed by Congress in 1806 provided for a national road running from Cumberland, Maryland, to the Ohio River, which passed through southwestern Pennsylvania and aided in developing that area. After 1790, anthracite coal was mined near Mauch Chunk (Jim Thorpe) and transported down the rivers to Philadelphia. Around 1800 iron was manufactured in Coatesville, Phoenixville, Lancaster, and the Juanita Valley. The Irish by the thousands began to settle in the mining areas upon the opening of the mines.

UNITED STATES RELIGIOUS CONGREGATIONS
(1775-1776)

Congregational	668	Catholic	56
Presbyterian	588	Moravian	31
Episcopalian	495	Congregational - Separatist	24
Baptist	494	Mennonite	16
Friends	310	French Protestant	7
German Reformed	159	Sandemanian	6
Lutheran	150	Jewish	5
Dutch Reformed	120	Rogerene	3
Methodist	65	Others	31
		TOTAL	**3,228**

A brief Account of the
Province of Pennsylvania,
Lately Granted by the
KING,
Under the GREAT
Seal of England,
TO
WILLIAM PENN
AND HIS
Heirs and Affigns.

Since (by the good Providence of *God*, and the Favour of the *King*) a Country in *America* is fallen to my Lot, I thought it not lefs my Duty, then my Honeft Intereft, to give fome publick notice of it to the World, that thofe of our own or other Nations, that are inclin'd to Tranfport Themfelves or Families beyond the Seas, may find another Country added to their Choice; that if they fhall happen to like the Place, Conditions, and Government, (fo far as the prefent Infancy of things will allow us any profpect) they may, if they pleafe, fix with me in the Province, hereafter defcribed.

I. *The* KING'S *Title to this Country before he granted it.*

It is the *Jus Gentium*, or Law of Nations, that what ever Wafte, or uncultured Country, is the Difcovery of any Prince, it is the right of that Prince that was at the Charge of the Difcovery: Now this *Province* is a Member of that part of *America*, which the King of *England's* Anceftors have been at the Charge of Difcovering, and which they and he have taken great care to preferve and Improve.

I. William

Title page of William Penn's *Brief Account*, 1682, whereby King Charles II of England presented William Penn with 28 million acres of land.

Portrait of William Penn.

Title page of Thomas Budd's *Tract*, printed by William Bradford, Philadelphia, Pennsylvania.

Good Order Eftablifhed
IN
Pennfilvania & New-Jerfey
IN
AMERICA,
Being a true Account of the Country;
With its Produce and Commodities there made.

And the great Improvements that may be made by means of Publick Store-houfes for Hemp, Flax and Linnen-Cloth; alfo, the Advantages of a Publick-School, the Profits of a Publick-Bank, and the Probability of its arifing, if thofe directions here laid down are followed. With the advantages of publick Granaries.

Likewife, feveral other things needful to be underftood by thofe that are or do intend to be concerned in planting in the faid Countries.

All which is laid down very plain, in this fmall Treatife; it being eafie to be underftood by any ordinary Capacity. To which the *Reader* is referred for his further fatisfaction.

By Thomas Budd.

Printed in the Year 1685.

AN EXPLANATION OF
SOME ACCOUNT OF THE PROVINCE OF PENNSYLVANIA

William Penn was very eager to advertise all the advantages of moving from the Old World to Pennsylvania. His eight written promotional tracts were "to give some public notice" of Pennsylvania "to the world." His brochures were not flashy, instead they were sober and restrained in tone. The printed word had real impact upon 17th century readers, thus he did not need to oversell or exaggerate.

His first promotional tract, *Some Account of the Province of Pennsylvania,* was written after Penn obtained his charter in March of 1681. Already widely known as a Quaker leader, he made no mention of his plans for a holy experiment or of his religion. William Penn hoped to appeal to a wide non-Quaker audience, and he sent this tract to friends throughout Wales, Scotland, England, and Ireland. It was quickly translated into German and Dutch. The description of the new land was brief and tips for packing and preparing for the journey were vague, since Penn had not yet been to Pennsylvania when he wrote this tract. His concentration was on improved family life, good government, a sense of adventure, material profits, and the acquisition of fertile land. His painted contrast between the decadent Old World and the hard-working innocence of the New World eventually became part of American literature.

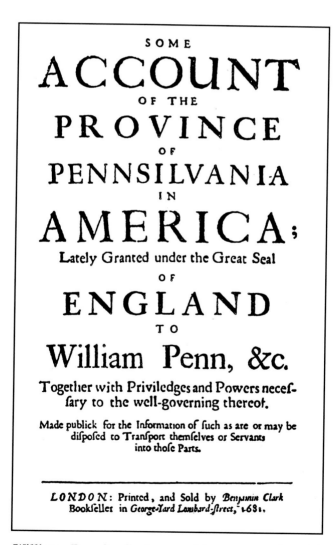

William Penn's first pamphlet concerning his American possessions.

SEVERAL KINDS OF BOND SERVANTS

Some people had scant means at the outset of their journey and arrived in Philadelphia virtually penniless and dependent. Upon their arrival, they were compelled to barter or sell personal services for a stated period of time. This was accomplished at a stipulated price, and under prescribed legal regulations. The debt was discharged to those in need of their labor, who were willing to discharge the debts in order that the immigrants reach this promised land, this modern Eden, in a new world.

As colonists in Pennsylvania, the first Germans to arrive were well-to-do. Nearly all of them had the means to pay the charges incurred going down the Rhine to the sea, plus meet the expenses to carry them across the ocean, and have money remaining when they arrived to pay for part or all of their land. Evidence of this are the large tracts purchased at Germantown and Conestoga. This was the rule until around 1717 when the great exodus from the Palatinate began. The poorer classes believed that America was a place where the poor might become rich. All the accounts that had been sent back were favorable concerning the ease by which land could be purchased, the soil's productiveness, the abundance of food, freedom from taxation, and the equality of all men before the law to their natural rights and their religious beliefs.

Their desire to flee from the land of oppression was paramount. To attain their wish, no hardship was too great or sacrifice too costly. Selling their humble belongings, they were able to proceed and reach a seaport. There they found men ready to assist them across the Atlantic, but the terms were hard. The suffering, maltreatment, and death on the voyage is one of the most pathetic pictures in the history of American colonization.

Persons without means, who came on the ships offered by shipmasters, were called "Redemptioners." The term does not appear in indentures entered between themselves and those who discharged their obligations in return for rendering personal services for a certain number of years. Such individuals, many from the British Isles, were called bond or indentured servants. These terms were known in the Province of Pennsylvania according to the Acts of the Assembly. The term was also a prevailing one in their mother country and followed them here.

There is a broad distinction between some of the indentured immigrants as they may be divided into two separate classes. The first consisted of good citizens and honest men. They came here of their own accord, had gone through trials at home because of their religion or the hard conditions of life from birth. Such people contracted terms of temporary servitude in a distant land in order to escape demanding taxes and possible starvation.

The other class did not come to America because of any special desire on their part. If they had a choice in the matter, doubtless they would have preferred to remain in their land of birth. These were the felons and criminals that the mother country had deluged upon her new Province to rid herself of an objectionable criminal class. Jails were emptied and inmates were sent to her colonies. Honest and industrious colonists in 1722 tried to prevent their coming by imposing a tax on every criminal that landed in the Province. They also made the shipowners responsible for the future conduct of his passengers. Nothing kept them out and the early criminal record in Pennsylvania is made from this class.

This group differed from the Germans seeking better living conditions, who were the flower of German peasantry. Europe boasted of no better citizens. These robust men worked the soil and were accustomed to earning a living with their hands. Their handiwork in Pennsylvania is a marvel of modern colonization. They were the commonwealth builders.

In spite of discouragement, deceit, wrong, and robbery, these peasant people still continued to come to a promised land. Shipboard treatment was horrible, and upon their arrival, money brokers stood ready to plunder and spoil. With their household treasures sold or stolen, thousands found themselves on Philadelphia's wharfs possessing only their lives and strong arms to begin anew the battle of life and a struggle for existence. Handicapped as they were, many faced their adverse fate and fulfilled their contracts with their masters faithfully.

Typical clothing worn by peasants from the Rhine Provinces known collectively as the Palatinate.

THE "REDEMPTIONER"
AND HIS VOYAGE ACROSS THE SEA

The word "Redemptioner" was originated as a system of voluntary servitude, recognized by law and custom. A free man entered into a contract with another person, to serve a stipulated time at a stipulated price, for money paid, in eight days or sooner. Ships were sometimes detained in port for eight to 14 days before their cargoes were completed. During the delay, everyone was required to spend his last money consuming the remaining stock of provisions reserved for the ocean voyage.

During the voyage, many died miserably from salted and spoiled food, the lack of food and medication, and foul water. Problems that had to be dealt with included stench, fumes, vomiting, fever, numerous diseases, dysentery, constipation, headache, boils, scurvy, cancer mouth-rot, hunger, thirst, heat, cold, dampness, anxiety, and lice.

The healthy grew impatient, cursing themselves or others for ever undertaking the journey. Sometimes they came near to killing each other while others would rob and cheat. Frequently children cried out against their parents, husbands against their wives, wives against their husbands, brothers and sisters, friends and acquaintances were also at each other.

Children ages one through seven rarely survived the voyage. Many parents saw their children die miserably and saw them cast into the water. On one ship, a witness viewed 32 children buried at sea.

It was not surprising that most got sick or died since warm food was only served three times per week. The meals were difficult to eat because they were so unclean. The water served was black, thick and full of worms. Often biscuits were consumed that were spoiled and full of red worms and spider nests.

After a long and tedious journey, with land in sight, the people went below the deck to see the land from afar. They wept for joy, prayed and sang, and thanked and praised God.

No one was permitted to leave the ships in Philadelphia after they landed except those who paid for their passage or gave good security. All the others remained on board until they were purchased and released from the ship by their purchasers. The sick fared the worst; the healthy were naturally preferred and purchased first.

Thousands of immigrants, after spending years freeing themselves and their loved ones, had to begin life anew. Generally their remaining years were crowned with abundance. At last they had attained their early hopes and now a period of fruition had arrived. Only men, women, and children deeply imbued with the consolations of religion could have survived it all!

Irish Redemptioner's Indenture dated 1784.

PASSAGE MONEY DUE BY REDEMPTIONERS

Noted here is an announcement from *Bradford's Journal* dated September 29, 1773 concerning unpaid passage money by German passengers arriving in the Philadelphia port.

"GERMAN PASSENGERS"

"Just arrived in the ship *Britannia,* James Peter, Master. A number of healthy GERMAN PASSENGERS, chiefly young people, whose freights are to be paid Joshua Fisher and Sons, or to the Master on board the Ship lying off the draw-bridge."

This ship had reached Philadelphia 11 days before the advertisement appeared in the newpaper. At this particular time, the Redemptioner market was not very brisk, therefore special efforts were required to work off the human cargo.

The partial list of passengers was prepared in the office of Messrs. Joshua Fisher & Sons, listing the amount of passage money due by each person, plus additional expenses for provisions, and so forth.

Andreas Keym	26.7	pounds
His wife, Lena Bekker	22.2	
Expenses for 16 days	1.12	
	50.1	pounds
John Frederick Camerloo	23.15	pounds
His wife, Anna	22.1	
Expenses	1.12	
	47.8	pounds
Hendrick Soueau	20.15	pounds
His wife, Dorothea	20.11	
Expenses	1.12	
	42.18	pounds

Augustinus Hess	19.1	pounds
His wife, Maria	18.19	
Daughter, Anna Margtta	19.4	
Expenses	2.8	
	59.12	pounds
Jacob Steyheler	19.19	pounds
His wife, Catharina	17.18	
Expenses	1.12	
	39.9	pounds
Christian Nell	20.0	pounds
Expenses	.16	
	20.16	
Conrad Foltz		
His wife, Susanna	51	pounds
Daughter, Maria		combined
Expenses	2.8	
	53.8	pounds
Jacob Wanner	20.15	pounds
His wife, Maria		combined
Expenses	1.12	
	22.7	pounds
Johann Jeremiah Snell	24.19	pounds
Expenses	.16	
	25.15	
Gerrett Benenge	23.11	pounds
Expenses	.16	
	24.7	pounds
Pierie Mullott	21	pounds
Expenses	.16	
	21.16	pounds

NEWSPAPERS' TESTIMONIES
CONCERNING TRAFFIC IN REDEMPTIONERS

Christopher Saur the Elder, a famous Germantown printer and publisher, was a sincere and faithful friend to the Redemptioners. Being present around the city of Philadelphia enabled him to be acquainted on a day-to-day basis with the activities among these unfortunate people. He took it upon himself as a publisher of a German newspaper to keep this human traffic before the public in his columns. His paper, *Der Hoch Deutsche Pennsylvanische Berichte*, related the coming of vessels, the condition of the immigrants, the seasons of arrival, and the treatment of the passengers on the trip.

Saur's columns stirred up the public so that they might seek better conditions for the German Redemptioner immigrants. Shown here are excepts from his newspaper plus extracts from an English paper called *The American Weekly Mercury*.

The American Weekly Mercury, Philadelphia,
    September 1, 1720:

"On the 30 (arrived) the ship *Laurel* John Coppel, from Leverpool and Cork with 240 odd Palatinate Passengers come here to settle."

(The above is the earliest record of any ship carrying Palatines I have found. Additional interest attaches to its arrival as it is most probably the vessel on which the well-known clergyman, Rev. J. Ph. Boehm, came to this country, August 30, 1720.)

The American Weekly Mercury, November 7, 1728:

"Just arrived from London, in the ship *Borden*, William Harbert, Commander, a parcel of young likely men servants, consisting of Husbandmen, Joyners, Shoemakers, Weavers, Smiths, Brickmakers, Bricklayers, Sawyers, Taylers, Stay-Makers, Butchers, Chair makers, and several other trades, and are to be sold very reasonable either for ready money, wheat Bread, or Flour, by Edward Hoone, in Philadelphia."

(The passengers were most probably English, Scotch, and Irish immigrants.)

The American Weekly Mercury, May 22, 1729:

"There is just arrived from Scotland, a parcel of choice Scotch Servants, Taylors, Weavers, Shoemakers and ploughmen, some for five and others for seven years; Imported by James Coults, they are on board a sloop lying opposite to the Market Street Wharf, where there is a boat constantly attending to carrying one on board that wants to see them."

Der Hoch Deutsche Pennsylvanische Berichte, Philadelphia, February 16, 1745:

"Another ship reached Philadelphia with 400 Germans and it is said not many over 50 remain alive. They received their bread ration every two weeks and many ate in 4, 5, and 6 days what should have done them 15 days. And when they get no cooked food for 8 days their bread was all so much the sooner; and when they had to wait 3 days over the three weeks, those without money became enfeebled, and those who had money could get plenty of flour from the captain, at three pence sterling per pound and a quart bottle of wine for seven thalers. A certain man whose wife was nearly famished bought every day meal and wine for her and their children, thus kept them alive: another man who had eaten all his week's bread asked the captain for a little bread, but in vain. He then came to the captain and requested the latter to throw them overboard at once rather than allow them to die by inches. He brought his meal sack to the captain and asked him to put a small quantity into it: the captain took the bag, put in some sand and stones and returned it to the man. The latter shed some tears, laid down and died, together with his wife."

The Pennsylvania Berichte, Philadelphia, August 1, 1749:

"A letter has been received in Germantown, written in the beginning of August, 1749, in Virginia, in which two potters say they sailed from Rotterdam for Philadelphia. Their company contracted with the Captain of the ship to pay ten doubloons for their passage, but he deceived them and carried them all to Virginia, and sold them for five years. They ask whether there is no help for them, as they never entered into such a contract. It appears the ship belonged to the Captain and was not consigned to any agent in Philadelphia."

The Pennsylvania Berichte, Germantown, November 16, 1749:

"The ships on which so many persons had put their chests, and which were so long in coming over, arrived on the 9 and 11 of the present month in Philadelphia. We hear that many of these chests were broken open. It is customary that when a ship captain receives goods and wares for delivery, he must turn them over to the owner as he receives them when the freight is paid, and what is lacking must be made good by him. But the Germans pay and must pay when their chests are robbed or when famished with hunger, even though their contracts are expressly to the contrary."

The Pennsylvania Berichte, No. 123, August 16, 1750:

"Six ships with Irish servants have arrived at Philadelphia, and two ships with German Newcomers. Some say 18 more are on their way here; others say 24 and still others 10,000 persons."

The Pennsylvania Berichte, Boston, September 25, 1752:

"On last Tuesday a ship arrived from Holland with 300 Germans, men, women, and children. Some of them will settle in Germantown, and the rest in the eastern part of the Province. There were 40 births on board during the voyage. Among the mechanics and artists were a great many glass workers, and a factory will be established for them as soon as possible."

The Pennsylvania Berichte, October 16, 1752:

"From a letter received from Charlestown, South Carolina, we learn that a vessel reached that harbor after a voyage of 18 weeks' duration. The people were all suffering from hunger and thirst. Another vessel that came from Rotterdam by way of Liverpool, also arrived with a cargo of Palatines, all of whom were fresh and well. When the Captains are stingy and save the money that should be used in buying provisions, the poor passengers die

of starvation, while their friends must pay for their deaths. If however the Captains are liberal and buy sufficient food, then it is just to pay for the food."

The Pennsylvania Berichte, September 16, 1755:

"Many Redemptioners having joined the army in Philadelphia, they will again be delivered to their former masters. They are sharply questioned whether they are servants, but when they declared they are not, when they really are, they are whipped."

The Pennsylvania Staatsbote, November 9, 1764:

"To-day the ship Boston, Captain Mathem Carr, arrived from Rotterdam, with several hundred Germans. Among them are all kinds of mechanics, day laborers and young people, men as well as women, and boys and girls. All those who desire to procure such servants are requested to call on David Rundle, on Front Street."

The Pennsylvania Staatsbote, January 18, 1774:

"GERMAN PEOPLE."

"There are still 50 or 60 German persons newly arrived from Germany. They can be found with the widow Kriderin, at the sign of the Golden Swan. Among them are two Schoolmasters, Mechanics, Farmers, also young children as well as boys and girls. They are desirous of serving for their passage money."

NUMBER OF GERMAN IMMIGRANT SHIPS
THAT ARRIVED IN THE PORT OF PHILADELPHIA
(1727-1775)

Year	Number	Year	Number	Year	Number
1727	5	1743	9	1759	None
1728	3	1744	5	1760	None
1729	2	1745	None	1761	1
1730	3	1746	2	1762	None
1731	4	1747	5	1763	4
1732	11	1748	8	1764	11
1733	7	1749	21	1765	5
1734	2	1750	14	1766	5
1735	3	1751	15	1767	7
1736	3	1752	19	1768	4
1737	7	1753	19	1769	4
1738	16	1754	17	1770	7
1739	8	1755	2	1771	9
1740	6	1756	1	1772	8
1741	9	1757	None	1773	15
1742	5	1758	None	1774	6
				1775	2

A total of 321 ships crossed the Atlantic Ocean during the 44-year span. We can note how the tide of immigration ebbed and flowed throughout the various years. The 40 shillings law (head tax) equal to $10.00 would have had a restraining effect on the poorest class which already endured severe financial strains.

Passenger ship about 1750.

SOME SHIPS CARRYING IMMIGRANTS TO THE PORT OF PHILADELPHIA IN 1738

Ship's Name	Arrival Date	Number of Passengers
Catharine	July 27	15
Winter Gallery	September 5	252
Glasgow	September 9	349
Two Sisters	September 9	110
Robert and Oliver	September 11	320
Queen Elizabeth	September 16	300
Thistle	September 19	300
Nancy and Friendship	September 20	187
Nancy	September 20	150
Fox	October 12	95
Davy	October 25	180
Saint Andrew	October 27	300
Bilender Thistle	October 28	152
Elizabeth	October 30	95
Charming Nancy	November 9	200
Enterprise	December 6	120

Frequently, two ships came into the port of Philadelphia on the same day. Three vessels landed on September 3, 1739, September 16, 1751, and again on September 27, 1752. All records were beaten when four immigrant ships arrived in Philadelphia on September 30, 1754.

Sixty-seven ships arrived between the years 1737 and 1746. They carried about 15,000 Germans who nearly all sailed from Rotterdam. There were 70 different ships out of the first 100 that brought immigrants to America. The *Samuel* made six trips; the *Saint Andrew,* four; the *Royal Judith,* five, and the *Friendship,* five. Names continued on the lists for many years. Some were classified as ships, others ranked as vessels, still others were known by names no longer in use by sea-faring men and shipbuilders, such as "billenders," "pinks," "snow," "brigs," and "brigantines."

Ship sizes by which immigrants reached Pennsylvania and the port at Philadelphia varied greatly. The smallest were around 63 feet in length over the gun deck, 20 feet 11 inches breadth of beam, and 9 feet 7½" inches at the depth of hold, carrying 109 tons. The largest deck measured 99 feet 8 inches, 26 feet 5 inches breadth of beam, and had a 312 ton capacity.

During some given years, the immigrants nearly all came from the Palatinate. Others flocked together such as the Saxons, Wurtembergers, Alsatians, and Hannoverians. Coming from the same locale, they desired to settle together upon their arrival. Other ships are known to have been composed of subjects from half a dozen German rulers.

Rotterdam was the principal port of embarkation, then on to Cowes, and the Isle of Wight. On occasion ships would load at London, but the numbers were small. Some points of departure were Leith, Deal, Plymouth, Portsmouth, Hamburg, and Cowes.

During and immediately following the close of the Revolutionary War, there was very little German immigration. According to the British Consul at Philadelphia, the numbers arriving between 1783 and 1789 were placed at 1,893 or an average of about 315 per year.

SEEKING A NEW IDENTITY

The Pennsylvania Dutch in their visionary attempt to form a utopia in America reflected upon their optimism, enthusiasm, and inner faith to create a suitable economic arena and a pleasing physical habitat. Their choices of names for communities reveals a vigorous strain of self-improvement and upward aspiration. Scanning of a Pennsylvania map will bring to mind their religious mission in America as we discover numerous inspirational names for their towns, including: Acme, Arcadia, Blooming Valley, Churchtown, Concord, Edenville, Effort, Enterprise, Fairhope, Freedom, Freeland, Frugality, Harmony, Homestead, Independence, Industry, Liberty, Lords Valley, Mount Joy, Mount Pleasant, New Freedom, New Hope, New Jerusalem, Paradise, Paradise Valley, Philadelphia (City of Brotherly Love), Pleasant Gap, Pleasant Mount, Pleasant Unity, Pleasant Valley, Progress, Prosperity, Salem (Peace), Unityville, and Zion.

SEQUENTIAL WAVES OF IMMIGRATION BY PERIODS

Encompassing more than 360 years of foreign immigration into the United States, this survey suggests five distinct divisional periods. Period I may be compared to cultural infancy, Period II to childhood and Periods III, IV, and V to adolescence and mature development.

Period I, (1607 - 1700): Initially there was a strong wave of English and Welsh, along with a major group of Africans.

Period II, (1700 - 1775): This movement was predominately an English, Welsh, and African assemblage. There were strong Teutonic and Scotch-Irish complements as well.

Period III, (1820 - 1870): This was the Northwest European wave which was heavily Irish, British, Dutch, and Teutonic, but also included other European groups plus some Asians, Canadians, and Latin Americans.

Period IV, (1870 - 1920): A great deluge with large numbers of eastern and southern Europeans and Scandinavians joining those from Northwestern Europe. Significant in quantity were Canadians, Asians, and Latin Americans.

Period V, (1920 to the present): A miscellaneous influx, less than the preceding period but of a major magnitude coming from western and southern Europe, Canada, Latin America, some Asian countries, as Latin America registered especially steady and major gains.

MUSEUMS

As an aid in differentiating numerous other types of china manufactured in England, Scotland, and Wales from Gaudy Dutch and Welsh, I have listed a variety of museums where one may go to study and view the similarities and differences evoked by many manufacturers.

ENGLISH LUSTREWARES (Early 19th Century)
Great Britain
Barlaston: Wedgwood Museum (Appointment necessary)
Cambridge: Fitzwilliam Museum
London: British Museum, Victoria and Albert Museum
Newcastle: Laing Art Gallery and Museum
Norwich: Castle Museum
Sunderland: Public Museum and Art Gallery
United States
Washington, DC: Smithsonian Institute
Winterthur, DE: Henry Francis du Pont Winterthur Museum

SWANSEA AND NANTGARW POTTERY AND PORCELAIN
Great Britain
Cardiff: National Museum of Wales
London: Victoria and Albert Museum
Swansea: Glynn Vivian Art Gallery, Royal Institution of South Wales

NEW HALL PORCELAIN
Great Britain
Bristol: City Art Gallery
Leeds: City Art Gallery
London: Victoria and Albert Museum

Port Sunlight: Lady Lever Art Gallery
Stoke-on-Trent: City Museum and Art Gallery, Hanley
Wolverhampton: Municipal Art Gallery and Museum

BRISTOL HARD PASTE PORCELAIN
Great Britain
Bath: Holburne of Menstrie Museum, Victoria Art Gallery
Bedford: Cecil Higgin Art Gallery
Bristol: City Art Gallery
Cambridge: Fitzwilliam Museum
Edinburgh: Royal Scottish Museum
London: British Museum, Victoria and Albert Museum
Luton: Luton Hoo
Plymouth: City Museum and Art Gallery
Truro: County Museum and Art Gallery

LONGTON HALL PORCELAIN
Great Britain
Bedford: Cecil Higgins Art Gallery
Cambridge: Fitzwilliam Museum
Leeds: Temple Newsam House
London: British Museum, Victoria and Albert Museum
Stoke-on-Trent: City Museum and Art Gallery, Hanley
United States
Boston: Boston Museum of Fine Arts
Seattle: Seattle Art Museum

ENGLISH ENAMELS
Great Britain
Bilston, Staffs: Museum and Art Gallery
London: Victoria and Albert Museum
Wolverhampton: Municipal Art Gallery and Museum

WORCESTER PORCELAIN
Great Britain
Bath: The Holburne Menstrie Museum of Art
Bedford: Cecil Higgins Art Gallery
Bristol: City Museum
London: British Museum, Victoria and Albert Museum
Worcester: Dyson Perrins Museum

LOWESTOFT PORCELAIN
Great Britain
Cambridge: Fitzwilliam Museum
Great Yarmouth: South Quay Museum
Ipswich: Christchurch Mansion
London: British Museum, Victoria and Albert Museum
Lowestoft: Public Library
Norwich: Castle Museum

CHELSEA PORCELAIN
Great Britain
Bedfordshire: Cecil Higgins Art Gallery
Bedford: Luton Hoo
Cambridge: Fitzwilliam Museum
London: British Museum, Victoria and Albert Museum
United States
Boston: Boston Museum of Fine Arts

BOW PORCELAIN
Great Britain
Leicester: Museum and Art Gallery
London: British Museum, London Museum, Victoria
    and Albert Museum
Edinburgh: Royal Scottish Museum
United States:
Providence: Rhode Island School of Design,
        Lucy Truman Aldrich Collection

AMERICAN PORCELAIN AND IMPORTED PIECES
Great Britain
Bath: American Museum in Britain, Claverton Manor
London: Victoria and Albert Museum
United States
West Chester, PA: West Chester Historical Society
New York: Metropolitan Museum of Art
Washington, DC: Smithsonian Institution
Williamsburg, VA: Colonial Williamsburg
Winterthur, DE: H.F. duPont Winterthur Museum
Dearborn, MI: Henry Ford Museum and
        Greenfield Village

Here is another list of recommended museums and collections in Great Britain where you may wish to travel and learn about a variety of pottery and porcelain types.
Glasgow: Art Gallery and Museum,
        The Burrell Collection
London: Bethnall Green Museum,
        The Museum of London,
        Sir Percival David Foundation, University of London;
        The Wallace Collection, Hertford House
Hastings: Hastings Museum and Art Gallery,
        Cambridge Road
Brighton: The Willet Collection,
        Art Gallery and Museum

RECOGNIZING GAUDY WELSH

1. There was no strict placement on designs featuring the same pattern since all of the artistic renderings were done by hand.

2. The majority of artists were right-handed, evidenced by their brush strokes. Much of the decorating was accomplished through the skills of women and children.

3. Many of the strokes were accomplished with thick brushes since they are wide and bold. Fine lines were done with very thin brushes.

4. Colors frequently encountered are the cobalt blues which often ran, found under the glaze. Typical colors include rust or burnt orange, pink, pink luster, yellow, green, and sometimes copper luster and turquoise.

5. Both sagging and pitting will be noted on some examples.

6. The body of the ware may be earthenware, creamware, ironstone, or bone china.

7. Thickness and weights vary considerably in Gaudy Welsh.

8. The ware may run the gamut from being opaque to being translucent.

9. The number of patterns produced in Gaudy Welsh probably approaches 300.

10. Generally you may discover pattern numbers on the bottoms of cups and saucers ranging from "2" to "4011." Other shapes may also be found with numbers.

11. Transfers were used and incorporated in some patterns, but this is an exception to the rule.

12. Gaudy Welsh was patterned after Japanese Imari.

13. The designs on Gaudy Welsh are colorful, free flowing, and unpretentious.

14. Gaudy Welsh was fabricated for the working class in Britain and the United States who could not afford the better china.

15. It is probable that manufacturers knew the patterns by numbers and Americans assigned names to them.

16. This ware was produced from 1820 to about 1860.

17. Gaudy Welsh originally sold for a few pennies per piece. Today its price range is from medium to high.

18. Today Gaudy Welsh is found widely scattered and collected throughout the United States.

19. Stilt or tripod marks are commonly found on the underside of flat examples.

20. Body styles in Gaudy Welsh are quite numerous.

21. Handles, finials, lids, and feet are extremely varied in Gaudy Welsh.

22. Flower petals usually are oval or rounded and their burnt orange coloration is shaded.

23. The grape leaf in blue is repeated often throughout the menagerie of patterns.

24. Sprigs and veined leaves appear on many Gaudy Welsh designs.

25. Many patterns have blue panelled borders with cartouches that number from three to seven.

26. Patterns without cartouches are usually complimented with scrolls or other repeated blue figures.

27. The fence, an oriental characteristic, appears on some patterns including Oyster and Dogwood.

28. Most Gaudy Welsh cups have interior designs. A few patterns also have exterior designs.

29. Some jugs and tea sets, such as Glamorgan, Dyfed, Anglesey and Wagon Wheel, have vertical stripes in their designs.

30. Gaudy Welsh was produced in many grades over the years, from very inferior to extremely well done.

PATTERN NUMBERS ASSOCIATED
WITH PATTERN NAMES

Listed are pattern numbers discovered on cups and saucers that will assist the reader in absolute identification when there is a doubt about a pattern's name. Unfortunately the list is not complete for all 125 patterns.

Name	Pattern	Name	Pattern
Asian	158	Oriental	113
Berma	232	Pansy	44
Cardiff	97	Peach	405
Carousel	822	Pennant	402
Cherry Tree	214	Peony	103
Chintz	929	Pink Rose	396
Columbine	2, 45, 111	Poppy	368
Daisy	123	Primrose	280
Drape	1102	Rainbow	3, 28
Dutch Rose	59	Ribbon	402
Esopus	2	Scallop	3100, 3101
Feather	153	Seguarro	38
Floret	293	Sheridan	958
Flower Basket I	31	Shrimp	10
Flower Basket II	291	Sunflower	30, 36, 1101
Fondant	3014	Tricorn	101
Fruit	1111	Urn II	106
Geranium	72	Venus	408, 807
Grape I	4011	Village	281, 282
Grape and Lily	480	Vine I	13
Herald	700	Vine II *(Note that these 2 variations have the same*	60, 719
Hexagon	603	Vine III *pattern numbers.)*	60, 719
Honeysuckle	67	Water Lily	32
Hudson	605	Welsh Warbonnet	15
Lotus	60, 150	Wisteria	2
Nightingale	358		

Discrepancies exist in some of the pattern numbers which may be attributed to careless mislabeling at the factory or coincidentally, two firms using the same pattern numbers. Examples are as follows: Vine II and Vine III, patterns 60 and 719; Lotus, Vine II, and Vine III, pattern 60; Esopus, Wisteria, and Columbine, pattern 2; and Pennant and Ribbon, pattern 402.

ALPHABETICAL LISTING OF
125 KNOWN GAUDY WELSH PATTERNS

Listed below are the patterns discovered while researching this portion of the text. There are perhaps other patterns to be discovered, and the list might be well over 200 and even exceed 300. Some names suggest geographic regions, numerous references are made to flowers, others deal with objects and specific shapes, and some of the names are very difficult to pronounce. The descriptions and definitions were added as an additional means of association and identification. Colors include blue, burnt orange, rust, green, yellow, pink, and luster.

Aberystwyth: This pattern possesses blue cartouches with white round and pierced rosettes, shaded flowers and leaves on branches compliment the design. County seat of Cardiganshire, Wales on the Cardigan Bay, population 10,000.

Anemone: Central is a large flower with nine blue scallops surrounded in an orange scallop, shaded orange buds, green leaves, plus blue stems and leaves complete the pattern. Also called "windflower," consisting of various plants having white, purple, or red cup-shaped flowers.

Anglesey: Parallel blue panels alternate with joined meandering and undulating lines. An island, 275 square miles in area, off the northwestern coast of Wales, population 58,000, county seat - Holyhead.

Asian: Blue eight-sided center has six-sided orange flower with a blue center, four rayed flowers project outward from the scalloped center, each has two blue leaves, border is made up of fine branch-like lines and four orange mounds with blue outlines, mounds have fine white designs. A term pertaining to Asia or its people.

Begonia: Has a scalloped blue border, clusters of three lobed leaves in blue, plus orange and green leaves, and large shaped orange florals appearing like a child's whirligig. Various plants native to the tropics, having brightly colored or veined and irregular leaves and various colored waxy flowers.

Bethesda: Central is a graduated three column pot with parallel lines which contains three types of florals in and around the design. A location in northern Wales, population 4,180.

Billingsley Rose: Possesses a wide blue border with two rose cartouches with two pink roses each plus two green triangular shapes. The center shows one pink rose surrounded by ten green leaves.

Bryn Pistyll: Left to right are blue and orange swirls with shaded elliptical three buds on a stem between each.

Buckle: There are three blue border strips with flowers and leaves between each, a blue buckle shape is part of the central motif.

Butterfly: Three large blue scalloped butterflies appear with lustered veins. There are shaded five-lobed flowers, vines, and tiny green leaves.

Caernarfon (Caernarvon?): This pattern is formed of orange shaded pansy-like florals with blue hearted centers, three joined blue obovate leaves, and a shaded orange six-divisioned shell-like form in the background. A county of Wales, 569 square miles in the northwest, population 122,000.

Cambrian Rose: A pointed blue lustered bat wing shape with an orange oval in its center, radiating from its base are orange tendrils to the left and right with blue lustered leaves, orange buds and small green leaves. Above the winged form is a blue nine-lobed shape with lustered veins, a large four-petaled heart-shaped flower has white orange veined leaves just above the flower. Pertaining to Wales; Welsh.

Cardiff: A 10-petaled orange flower is central to the design, fine orange vines with green leaves and orange flowers radiate throughout the pattern. Major port and industrial city of Wales on the Bristol Bay, population 260,000.

Carmarthen: Two half-moon shapes are spaced at the base with the addition of branches, leaves, and varied shaded grape-shaped flower clusters. A county of Wales, 919 square miles in the southwest, population 168,000.

Carousel: Five angular pole-like forms jut toward the russet lobed central flower giving a whirling motion to the pattern.

Castle Medallion: This pattern has two large shaded leaves around the edge plus two castle designs inside two blue scalloped cartouches.

Centerpiece: Central to the pattern is a six-petaled stemmed flower with shaded lobes surrounded to the left and right by blue clustered leaves in groups of five.

Cherry Tree: Four blue scallops are at the base and the trunk of the tree grows from here. The branches and fruit radiate around the edge.

Chinoisserie (Chinoiserie?): This pattern has a wide blue border with two cartouches showing an oriental done with a transfer, two narrow pointed russet shapes are on the border. The central panel shows an oriental with an umbrella (transfer) surrounded by trees. An art style reflecting Chinese influence through the use of elaborate decorations and intricate patterns.

Chintz: Wide blue border with the addition of three wider half scallops, yellow centered flower outlined in orange is central in the pattern. Multicolored, bright.

Clwyd: Consists of oval shaded flowers on branches with three white shaded lobed petals.

Columbine: Possesses a wide blue lustered border, three cartouches with small pink and orange flowers, green leaves and has a similar central flower. Any of several plants having variously colored flowers with five conspicuously spurred petals, dovelike.

Cosmos: Wide blue lustered border, three cartouches, and orange and pink flowers in each surrounded by green foliage. Central is one pink flower and green leaves. Various tropical American plants having variously colored rayed flowers, used as a garden plant.

Covered Urn: Central motif is ornately lustered blue urn, overlapping blue leaves and burnt orange flowers are shown, a cluster of rock forms outlined in blue is also shown.

Crest: Three blue crests appear on the border, spaced between each is a scroll and a shaded flower with five petals.

Cyclamon II (Cyclamen?): Shown is a predominance of blue veined serrated leaves and blue tendrils plus two blue ovals topped with an oval orange bud, additional green leaves are present. Any of several plants having showy white, pink, or red flowers with reflexed petals, also called "sowbread."

Daisy: Wide blue lustered edging with three cartouches having pink petaled florals with green leaves on two sides. The central motif shows a single flower of the same type with leaves. Also called "English daisy" or "bachelor's button." The flowers have yellow centers and pink or white rays.

Daisy and Chain: A variant of the daisy pattern. (See Daisy.)

Deiniolen: Harp-shaped panels contain a central cluster of five round and shaded petals with stems and leaves.

Dimity: Center consists of white five-petaled flower with a touch of orange plus a yellow center. A scrolled six-lobed blue border exposes florals and green leaves in the white outside edged panels. A sheer, crisp cotton fabric, usually corded or checked.

Dogwood (Shanghai): This pattern has two shaded five-petaled flowers with vines and leaves in blue. Any of several trees or scrubs having small greenish flowers surrounded by showy white or pink bracts that resemble petals.

Dotted Circle: The blue border has three floral cartouches with three flowers each in orange, a concentric orange centered ring has 13 orange dots.

Drape: Four blue drapes on the edge are spaced between orange serrated shapes. There is a triangular and veined three-lobed center leaf plus ornate and shaded pinwheel flowers in orange.

Drysau: Shown are rectangular columns with arched tops in blue luster which display alternating orange lines and wiggly green lines between the columns, orange shaded buds complete the pattern.

Ducks: This pattern displays blue ducks amid rushes and five-petaled shaded flowers.

Dutch Rose: An orange shaded twelve overlapping petaled flower is in the center, six blue fern-like shapes project from the edge grouped in twos, three five-petaled orange flowers are around the edge. There are additional fine green leaves and orange buds. (See Pink Rose.)

Dyfed: There are vertical blue panels with rust scalloped shading and green leaves between each panel.

Elfin Cap: Three blue elf-like caps dominate the center of the design plus orange flowers and crescents, three orange crescents are on the outside of the complex blue border which is lobed and six-sided. Small, sprightly. Pertaining to or of the nature of an elf.

Eryri: This pattern has fancy fencing, slash marks, buds and stems, plus a six-petaled shaded flower with buds.

Esopus: Six octopus blue rays radiate inward from the narrow blue border. Six outside panels contain alternating three and four orange flowers with green leaves. In the center is a single orange flower.

Feather: Displays a wide blue border with three cartouches having pink feather-like forms. The central motif is the same feather.

Floret: A wide blue lustered border has three floral cartouches containing pink flowers with yellow centers plus russet stems and green leaves. Central are pink flowers and yellow ones outlined in green. A small flower, usually part of a dense cluster; one of the disk or ray flowers, such as a daisy.

Flower Basket (I, II, and III): Orange florals and green leaves are found throughout this pattern. A handled flower basket is central to the design and is complimented by three scrolls and three flower baskets at the edges.

Fondant: Central to this pattern is a four-petaled orange flower with the addition of three five-petaled orange flowers with yellow centers surrounded by blue leaves.

Forget-Me-Not: Alternating panels show blue pipe-shaped forms underlined in orange. Above each is a cluster of shaded orange buds and daisy-shaped blue flowers having five petals each. Any of various low-growing plants having clusters of small blue flowers.

Fruit: There is a blue border and two scalloped cartouches with pink florals, two orange triangles point east and west on the border, a pink flower is in the center of the design.

Geranium: The pattern reveals three blue edged panels, shaded five-petaled flowers between each, and an orange eight-petaled central flower. Also called "cranesbill" - a variety of plants having divided leaves and pink or purplish flowers.

Glamorgan: Vertical colored panels are shown with crescent-shaped flowers and leaves between, interspersed on white sections. A county, 813 square miles in area in southeastern Wales, county seat - Cardiff, population 1,244,000. A mining and manufacturing district.

Gower: This pattern has four blue lobed edges, rosette flowers between each, bud-like orange floral is the central design.

Grape (I, II, III, IV, V, VI, VII, VIII, IX): The design is formed of shaded leaves and oval grape-like flowers and raindrop-like petals.

Grape and Lily: An ornate blue and burnt orange border is shown with a swirling blue vine, a grape cluster and orange lily and leaves are in the center of the design.

Gwent: Arched columns with five shaded and serrated flowers on a branch are alternately shown alongside of two flowers on a leafed branch with three pointed and shaded flowers.

Gwynedd: Shown are vertical blue and burnt orange panels with shaded lobe petals between each. A single blooming flower is below.

Gwyrfai: Vertical blue panels are present having green leaves and vertically joined burnt orange buds.

Herald: Centered is a four-sided lobed orange flower and a scalloped blue border with three orange trunk shapes with three white dots and white arched bases.

Hexagon (I, II): This pattern has a six-sided central motif with a flower plus leaves and veins outside on white, bordered by three half moon panels on the edge shaded blue and orange.

Honeysuckle: The center is comprised of a blue three leafed clover shape superimposed over an orange bud. Radiating from the center are three blue branched stems with leaves that break to the left and right. Between the branches are a four petaled orange flower and green leaves. Various shrubs or vines having tubular, often very fragrant white, yellowish or pink flowers.

Hudson: Three blue butterfly cartouches are along the edge with orange inside, counterbalanced in the center are two clusters of three blue leaves each with two orange buds, clusters of blue leaves and orange buds are between the cartouches.

Japan: An oriental house is central to the design with trees. There is a heavy blue border with four spaced orange flowers inside the blue border.

Leek: Shown here is an ornate blue scrolled border. Between each scroll are orange flowers, one flower is central to the pattern. A plant related to the onion and having a white, slender bulb and dark-green leaves.

Llanberis: Five ovate and shaded buds grow from a butterfly shape. Clusters of branches, buds and palmette leaves complete the pattern.

Llangefni: This pattern has large C-scrolled branches, reverse and obverse, that possess lobed leaves. Interspersed are rosette florals with nine lobes and also five-lobed shaded flowers.

Llanrug: Characteristic to this pattern are intertwining stems with hanging florals plus six shaded and veined oval leaves.

Lleyn: Four florals dominate this pattern: tulip shapes, three bud grape clusters, overlapping nine oval-petaled flowers, and five-petaled broadly pointed forms.

London: There are two concentric circles in the center of the design, scattered tiny leaves around the edge, plus eight shaded oval buds on stems.

Lotus: This pattern is made up of a blue over red center flower resembling a water lily. There are three similar large border flowers with lance-shaped green leaves. An aquatic plant native to southern Asia, having large leaves, fragrant pink flowers, and a broad, rounded, perforated seed pod.

Lyre: Easily recognizable is the blue lyre shape with four orange petals growing from it. Additional green leaves and blue lustered shapes compliment this pattern.

Marigold: An orange flower and green leaves are central to the pattern. The border consists of three blue triangles outlined in orange that touch the central six-sided blue scalloped outline, three orange flower groupings have four buds and six green leaves. This grouping includes several species of widely cultivated plants grown for their showy orange or yellow flowers.

Merioneth: Displayed is a large shaded five-petaled flower. Veined leaves radiate from the flower and there is also a blue butterfly shape with serrated wings.

Morning Glory: Four blue ragged-edged evergreen shapes radiate inward from the edge. Spaced between are seven-lobed orange flowers with blue heart centers on blue squiggly stems. Small green leaves are also spaced around the edge. A variety of twining vines having funnel-shaped, variously colored flowers that close late in the day.

Nebula: Possesses a wavy blue border with four lobed blue center. The white portion of the pattern contains two orange flowers opposite each other with five petals each. To the east and west are shaded orange flowers with blue centers.

Nightingale: This motif has a blue border, three russet and floral cartouches. A bird perched on a branch is central to the design.

Oriental: Centered is a blue hexagon with an orange flower. Three panels of orange with white dots are surrounded by a blue outline and also graces the edge.

Oyster (Blue Rock, Buddha, and Smoking Indian): This is a common pattern showing three blue lustered graduated rocks, fencing, and floral leaves and vines in blue and orange.

Pagoda: A blue pagoda shape with two orange doorways on a blue ground is central to the design. Flowering trees surround the pagoda. There is a narrow blue border interspaced with four orange buds.

Panelled Daisy: There is a round central panel with a single flower surrounded on the outside by three blue panels with flowers in between. (See Daisy.)

Pansy: There is a single blue scallop on the edge, blue stems and leaves flow from this source. There is a large orange flower and three smaller florals shown.

Peach: Shown are three scalloped borders in blue with a peach shape inside each. There are blue leaves and flowers throughout the pattern.

Peacock: Depicted here are florals and a plumed peacock with a fantail standing on a fence.

Pennant: This pattern is made up of three undulating blue flags with the added feature of two flowers between each.

Peony: Central to the pattern is a blue double-wing butterfly mound shape with large nine-petaled overlapping orange flower. There is the addition of five orange flower clusters and blue leaves around the edge. Any of various garden plants having large pink, red, white or creamy flowers.

Peppermint: This pattern possesses a pentagon-shaped blue border, five orange peppermint-like candy sticks radiate from each corner. There is a narrow green border between the clusters. Central is a shaded five-petal orange flower surrounded by five green petaled flowers having blue lustered centers. A plant having small purple or white flowers and downy leaves that yield a pungent oil.

Petunia: Central to this pattern is an orange shaded grape-like floral cluster with eight petals, blue serrated leaves, orange buds and numerous green leaves are part of this design also. Any of various widely cultivated plants native to South America having funnel-shaped flowers in colors from white to purple.

Pink Rose: Bordered in blue with three pink rose cartouches and three green elliptical forms. In the center is a large pink rose and green leaves highlighted in yellow. Numerous shrubs or vines usually having prickly stems, compound leaves and variously colored, often fragrant flowers.

Pinwheel: A pinwheel shape consisting of five blue and three orange flowers is central to this pattern. There are three blue scalloped borders with six-lobed orange and blue flowers between each.

Pontrhythallt: This pattern consists of a large shaded and veined, lobed and pointed four-petaled flower surrounded by shaded and lance-shaped leaves.

Poppy: Central to the pattern are two small green leaves, two blue lustered leaves topped with an orange shaded three-petaled tulip shape. The exterior design reveals three large oval poppies with orange centers, a blue middle section which is scalloped, and a scalloped exterior orange section. Blue vines, lustered blue leaves, green leaves, and shaded four-lobed orange flowers are interspersed between each of the large poppies. Any of numerous plants of the temperate regions, having showy red, orange, or white flowers.

Pot de Fleurs I: A variant of Pot de Fleurs II.

Pot de Fleurs II: This pattern shows a bulbous blue pot on an orange ground with blue stems, green leaves, white leaves outlined and veined, plus large orange lobed-shaped flowers.

Powys: Shown in this pattern are four rectangular cartouches with a fine multi-petaled flower superimposed. Below this design are orange petaled buds on stems facing to the left and right with additional fine stems, small green leaves and ornate ruffled flowers completing the pattern. A county in Wales, population 101,500.

Prestatyn: Central to this motif is an overlapping petaled flower and three-toed footprint-like leaves.

Primrose: In the center of this pattern is a shaded 11-lobed orange flower with tiny green leaves, assorted sized blue leaves and orange flowers complete this design.

Prince of Wales: There are blue lustered bat winged shapes with sharp serrated edges with orange superimposed. Additional green leaves, blue evergreen shapes and orange panels are also part of the pattern.

Rainbow: The center of the design is a blue hexagon with three half-moon rays around the outside edge having green and orange between the blue rays. Six burnt orange lobed flowers touch the central hexagon.

Repousse: Two blue half-moons occur at the base with a basket central to them. There are three equidistant flowers around the rest of the edge and a shaded six-petaled flower with leaves in the center.

Rhondda: There is a circular central panel with a shaded five-petaled flower. The edge of the panel has six crescent shapes plus three floral cartouches are shown around the outside edges with florals inside.

Rhymney: An artistically designed pattern. Central to the design are a symmetrically balanced cluster of leaves, and a five-petaled flower above with the addition of two stems covered with leaves and flowers.

Ribbon: A ribbon with two heart-shaped bows plus clusters of three blue leaves, green leaves, pink and burnt orange flowers are shown in this particular pattern.

Rocking Urn: A blue urn with orange flowers on a blue rocking chair base appears. Scattered throughout are leaves and three types of floral buds.

Rosemary: Three pointed and serrated blue mounds project from the edge. Between each are burnt orange buds and green leaves plus one orange five-petaled flower. An aromatic evergreen shrub of Southern Europe, having light blue flowers and grayish-green leaves that are used in cooking and perfume making.

Sahara: Four interspersed border panels contain one orange flower each having five petals plus orange buds and green leaves. Four blue lance-shaped panels tipped in orange radiate inward. The center contains a six-petaled orange flower with a blue "X" as its center.

Scallop: A six-sided scallop in blue is central with a floral center. Three blue mounds appear along the edge. There are bursts of orange flowers between each.

Seguarro: Three V-shaped designs in blue occur around the edge. There is a lighter blue on the outside and seven sparsely scattered florals.

Serenade: Five four-petaled and three-petaled orange flowers are shown in the center surrounded by green and blue leaves. The outside border is made up of four blue scrolls well spaced with green dots on a pink ground.

Sheridan: There are three blue-edged mounds with a narrow orange ribbon border between each, three orange flower forms touch the blue edge, and three additional blue florals outlined in orange touch the ribbons.

Shrimp: Pictured are two large orange shrimp shapes outlined in blue. Also shown are blue vines, russet flowers, and leaves.

Strawberry: This pattern reveals a blue border with a profusion of blue vines, green leaves, fruit and orange florals. A variety of low-growing plants having white flowers and red fleshy edible fruit.

Strawflower: The border is a wide blue. There are three winged cartouches with orange paramecium-shaped flowers and green leaves. This design is complimented in the center with the same two flowers surrounded by leaves. A plant native to Australia, having flowers with showy, variously colored bracts that retain their color when dried.

Sunflower: There is a blue scalloped base with a radiating vine covered with green leaves and small orange flowers. A central blue flower is outlined in russet. Any of several plants having tall, coarse stems and large yellow-rayed flowers that produce edible seeds rich in oil.

Tricorn: This pattern has a three-cornered scalloped blue border which encloses a white central pyramid shape with shaded orange eight-petaled flower in the midst. There are buds at each corner in orange.

Trumpet: Blue stemmed with two opposing blue leaves plus burnt orange trumpet-shaped flowers make this an easy pattern to recognize.

Tulip (I, II, III, IV, V, VI, VII, VIII): Three blue lobed pyramidal panels with luster radiating from the edge. Interspersed are tiny green and rust-colored leaves on russet stems. Ragged-edged tulips in yellow are outlined in burnt orange. Any of several bulbous plants native to Asia, widely cultivated for their showy, varied and colorful flowers.

Tyne: Fine green leaves are shown with a blue three-some of leaves north and south. Shaded burnt orange three-petaled flowers face east and west. A river of northern England, rising in eastern Cumberland and flowing 80 miles east to the North Sea.

Urn: This pattern reveals a fancy urn with florals and three serrated butterfly leaves above and to the left and right of the urn.

Venus: Central to the pattern is one orange flower surrounded by six green leaves. The border is wide and blue with four cartouches. Two are shaded pink, the other two have two small orange flowers surrounded by small green leaves.

Village: Six blue spokes radiate to the central design of two orange houses outlined in blue. There is a blue and orange ground.

Vine (I, II, III): There are three thin blue scalloped edges plus intertwining vines with shaded buds and a central flower.

Violet: Depicted here is a blue border with three five-sided cartouches. Orange florals and green leaves in the center are encircled with orange. A variety of low-growing plants having spurred, irregular flowers that are characteristically purplish-blue, yellow, and white.

Wagon Wheel: Rectangular blue lustered panels radiate about the object. Centered inside each panel are joined and alternating orange two toe-like tracks.

Water Lily: A blue lustered border projects inward shaped like an equilateral triangle with a wavy interior. Central to the pattern are orange bud clusters, green leaves, and a blue lustered leaf. A variety of plants with showy, colored, often trumpet-shaped flowers, native to ponds and lakes.

Welsh Warbonnet: A feathered warbonnet with luster is central to the motif. A profusion of blue lustered leaves, burnt orange flowers and small green leaves complete the pattern.

Wildflower: A large blue stemmed flower having lustered leaves and tulip-like buds with orange tips, plus the addition of narrow clusters of green leaves radiating outward from the blue stem make up this pattern. A flowering plant that grows in a natural, uncultivated state.

Wisteria: This design possesses a blue vine with five branches and leaves plus orange rosette and lobed clustered flower buds. Any of several climbing woody vines having compound leaves and drooping clusters of showy purplish or white flowers.

Wye: Central to the pattern and scalloped is a triangular three-sided form with a central four-petaled flower. An additional single flower is shown in each corner. There are panels of three broadly pointed flowers around the edge. A river on the border of England and Wales.

Yorkshire: The border has a wide blue bat wing design with six orange crescents well spaced. The central design contains an orange eight-spoked flower plus buds and green leaves.

Roman numerals behind a pattern name indicate a number of subtle variations found in the designs. Undoubtedly, many other variations exist.

VIEWING AND PURCHASING
GAUDY DUTCH AND GAUDY WELSH

Listed are numerous museums and historical societies where Gaudy Dutch and Gaudy Welsh may be viewed, studied, and enjoyed.

- Philadelphia Museum of Art,
    Philadelphia, Pennsylvania
- Henry Francis du Pont Winterthur Museum,
    Winterthur, Delaware
- Henry Ford Museum and Greenfield Village,
    Dearborn, Michigan
- Smithsonian Institute,
    Washington, District of Columbia
- Boston Museum of Fine Arts,
    Boston, Massachusetts
- New York Historical Society,
    New York, New York
- The Metropolitan Museum of Art,
    New York, New York
- Colonial Williamsburg,
    Williamsburg, Virginia

- Cooper-Hewitt Museum,
    New York, New York
- Cooper Union Museum for the Arts of Decoration,
    New York, New York
- Frick Collection,
    New York, New York
- Van Cortland Mansion and Museum,
    Bronx, New York, New York
- Annie. S. Kemerer Museum,
    Bethlehem, Pennsylvania
- Berks County Historical Society,
    Reading, Pennsylvania
- Historical Society of Montgomery County,
    Norristown, Pennsylvania

This list provides sources where you may inspect and purchase Gaudy Dutch and Gaudy Welsh and other fine china.

- Edward G. Wilson,
    1802 Chestnut Street, Philadelphia, Pennsylvania
- Freeman Fine Arts of Philadelphia,
    1808 Chestnut Street, Philadelphia, Pennsylvania
- Pennypacker Auction Centre, 1540 New Holland
    Road, Kenhorst (Reading), Pennsylvania
- Parke-Bernet Galleries, New York City
- Conestoga Auction, Manheim, Pennsylvania
- Steckel House Antiques,
    Northampton and Chestnut Streets,
    Bath, Pennsylvania on Routes 248 and 987
- Shawna Shop, Shawnee-on-the-Delaware, Pennsylvania
- Bea Cohen, P.O. Box 825, Easton, Pennsylvania
- Weber and Weber, Emmaus, Pennsylvania
- Richlandtown Antique Centre, Route 212 and Union
    Street, Richlandtown, Pennsylvania
- Renninger's Number One,
    Exit 21, Pennsylvania Turnpike,
    Adamstown, Pennsylvania
- Alderfer Auction Company,
    501 Fairgrounds Road, Hatfield, Pennsylvania
- Stephenson's Auction, 1005 Industrial Boulevard,
    Southhampton, Pennsylvania
- Leesport Antiques Mart, 162 North Center Avenue,
    Leesport, Pennsylvania
- North Gate Antique Mall, 726 North Hanover Street,
    Exit 16, Pennsylvania Turnpike,
    Carlisle, Pennsylvania

- Meadow View Antiques Co-Op,
    Route 322, Hershey, Pennsylvania
- Antique Market in Historic Gettysburg,
    Fourth and Water Streets,
    Gettysburg, Pennsylvania
- Clyde Youtz, Newmanstown, Pennsylvania
- Ed Stoudt's Antique Complex,
    Exit 21, Pennsylvania Turnpike,
    Adamstown, Pennsylvania
- Country Corner Antiques, Frog Hollow Farm, R.D. 5,
    Box 590, Boyertown, Pennsylvania
- Elizabeth Brady Antiques, Harrisburg, Pennsylvania
- Mae E. Smithers, 2400 Market Street,
    Harrisburg, Pennsylvania
- Black's Antiques,
    155 Village Street, Johnstown, Pennsylvania
- Fae B. Haight Antiques, Lahaska Antique Courte,
    Box 294, Lahaska, Pennsylvania
- Joyce M. Leiby,
    P.O. Box 6048, Lancaster, Pennsylvania
- Veronique's Antiques, 124 South Market Street,
    Mechanicsburg, Pennsylvania
- Charlotte Egan Antiques, Media, Pennsylvania
- The Lord and Tessler, 1A - 1B - 1C Kedron Avenue,
    Morton, Pennsylvania
- Ren's Antiques, 14 South State Street,
    Newtown, Pennsylvania
- Hollenbaugh's Antiques, Shiremanstown, Pennsylvania

- Sugarbush Antiques, 832 May Post Office Road, Strasburg, Pennsylvania
- Mary Delhamer, R.D. 9, Box 20, York, Pennsylvania
- Paul Ettline's Antiques, 3790 East Market Street, York, Pennsylvania
- Shupp's Grove Opening
  (Usually beginning in late April), one mile south of Adamstown, Pennsylvania on Route 897, two miles north of Lancaster-Reading interchange of the Pennsylvania Turnpike, Exit 21
- Kutztown, Pennsylvania Antique and Collector's Outdoor Extravaganza,
  over 1,200 dealers showing in late April, June, and September
- Log Cabin Antique Center, Denver, Pennsylvania, Route 272, just North of Pennsylvania Turnpike Exit 21
- Heritage I, Adamstown, Pennsylvania,
  One-half mile north of Pennsylvania Turnpike Entrance 21
- Heritage II, Reamstown, Pennsylvania,
  Two miles south of Pennsylvania Turnpike Exit 21
- Weaver's Antique Mall, Sinking Spring, Pennsylvania, One-mile north of Adamstown on Route 222
- The Antique Market at Phoenix Square on Third Street between Hamilton and Linden Streets, Allentown, Pennsylvania
- The Valley Shoppe Antiques, C.M. Brossman, East Earl, R.D. 1, Pennsylvania, 17519
- Sotheby's, 1334 York Avenue, New York City
- Sotheby's 34-35 New Bond Street, London, England
- Butterfield's, 1244 Sutter Street, San Francisco, California 94109
- Dunning Auction Service, 755 Church Road, P.O. Box 866, Elgin, Illinois 60121
- Jackson's Auction Gallery, 5330 Pendleton Avenue, Anderson, Indiana 46011

- David and Linda Arman, R.D. #1, Box 353A, Woodstock, Connecticut 06281
- William Doyle Galleries, 175 East 87th Street, New York, New York 10028
- Garth's Auction, Incorporated, 2690 Stratford Road, P.O. Box 369, Delaware, Ohio 43015
- Robert W. Skinner, Incorporated, Bolton Gallery, Route 117, Bolton, Massachusetts 01740
- Christie's, 502 Park Avenue, New York, New York 10022
- Christie's East, 219 East 67th Street, New York, New York 10021
- Christie's, 8 King Street, SW1Y 6QT, London, England
- Christie's, 8 Place de la Taconnerie, 1204 Geneve, Geneva, Switzerland
- Christie's, Cornelis Schuytstraat 57, 1071 JG, Amsterdam, Netherlands
- Leslie Hindman Auctioneers, 215 West Ohio Street, Chicago, Illinois 60610
- Phillips, 406 East 79 Street, New York, New York 10021
- Phillips, Blenstock House, 7 Blenheim Street, New Bond Street, W1Y OAS, London, England
- Bonnie Brae Auction Center, Route 724, 8 miles west of Valley Forge, Spring City, Pennsylvania
- Green Hills Auction Center, R.D. #4, Box 4471, midway between Routes 222 and 176, located on Route 568 south of Reading, Mohnton, Pennsylvania
- Brookwood Antiques, P.O. Box 8, Tallmadge, Ohio
- William R. and Teresa F. Kurau, P.O. Box 457, Lampeter, Pennsylvania
- The Green Tureen Antiques, 431 Bethlehem Pike, Fort Washington, Pennsylvania 19034

RESTORATION SOURCES

- Cunningham Antique Restoration, 422 West Plain View Road, Springfield, Missouri 65807
- David Jasper, P.O. Box 46, Lennox, South Dakota 57039
- Harry A. Eberhardt and Son, 201 Walnut Street, Philadelphia, Pennsylvania 19106
- Stewart Grady China Restoration, 2019 Sansom Street, Philadelphia, Pennsylvania 19103

- Ludwig A. Klein and Sons, Route 63, Harleysville, Pennsylvania 19438
- John E. Klein, 124 South 22nd Street, Philadelphia, Pennsylvania 19103
- Joe Howell, 416 Jefferson Street, Hagerstown, Maryland 21740
- Ronald L. Aiello, Antique Restorations, 1001 High Street, Burlington, New Jersey 08016

POTTERY AND PORCELAIN PUBLICATIONS

The list provided includes newspapers and magazines that devote some of their space to interesting articles and columns on pottery and porcelain.

The Connoisseur,
224 West 57th Street, New York, New York 10019

Antique Monthly,
P.O. Drawer 2, Tuscaloosa, Alabama 35402

Antiques and Auction News,
Route 230 West, Box 500,
Mount Joy, Pennsylvania 17552

West Coat Peddler,
P.O. Box 5134, Whittier, California 90607

The New York Antique Almanac,
Box 335, Lawrence, New York 11559

Maine Antique Digest,
P.O. Box 645, Waldboro, Maine 04572
Yesteryear,
Box 2, Princeton, Wisconsin 54968

Southern Antiques and Southern Trader,
P.O. Box 1550, Lake City, Florida 32005

Collector News,
Box 156, Grundy Center, Iowa 50638

Antique Review,
P.O. Box 538, Worthington, Ohio 43085

The Magazine Antiques,
551 Fifth Avenue,
New York, New York 10017

Antiques and Collecting Hobbies,
1006 South Michigan Avenue,
Chicago, Illinois, 60605

New York - Pennsylvania Collector,
Fishers, New York 14453

Antique Showcase,
Amis Gibbs Publications, Limited,
Canfield, Ontairo, Canada NOA 1CO

Antiques and The Arts Weekly,
5 Church Hill Road, Newton, Connecticut 06470

Antique Trader Weekly,
P.O. Box 1050, Dubuque, Iowa 52001

Antique Week - Tri-State Trader,
P.O. Box 90, Knightstown, Indiana 46148

GLOSSARY

Adam's Rose: Possesses a border of two red roses with green shoots. Manufactured by William Adams and Son, Tunstall and Stoke.

Allerton, Charles and Sons: Reproduced jugs in the Oyster pattern, Wagon Wheel design, and the Sunflower pattern. Worked from 1859 to 1942 at Park Works, Longton. Unmarked pieces reveal a cramped style and streaked, uneven red-orange pigments. Details and placement of designs are poorly executed.

Ball Clay: Has plasticity to hold its shape when formed and dry strength so that it does not chip and crack easily. A sedimentary clay with many organic impurities, in brown, blue, and black. These impurities are burned off at over 600 degrees Celsius.

Barge: Used as a method of transporting goods, barge captains paid to have dams (weirs) on the rivers opened so that they could float their barge to its destination. Later canals proved to be a better alternative.

Blunging: A process of removing impurities from the clay by breaking it into pieces and mixing with water. As a slip solution, the impurities fall to the bottom and the clay is poured into a sieve to get rid of other non-essentials. The moist clay was then passed through a heated trough to vaporize the water.

Bone China: Expensive to manufacture because of the kiln loss and the cost of ingredients. Fired at 1,000 degrees Celsius to stablize, glazed and refired at 1,250 degrees Celsius revealing a white and translucent body that is damage resistant. Its ingredients as produced by Spode in the 19th century included 52 parts bone ash, 24 parts china clay, and 24 parts Cornish stone.

Brighton Pavilion: A tribute to the reign of King George IV, this monument had a classical exterior that was changed by John Nash to an East Indian design. The lavish interior was furnished in the Chinese style as George's tastes in porcelain leaned toward Japanese patterns.

Cambrian Pottery: Located in Swansea and founded in 1764 making redware, the firm's trends changed when George Haynes went into partnership with one of the sons in the late 1780's. Later William Dillwyn in 1802 controlled the pottery, then the management passed to his son, Louis Weston Dillwyn. In 1814, the Nantgarw porcelain factory was founded in Swansea. After 1824, earthenware and Gaudy Welsh was produced. Red, veined leaves plus the impressed mark "Dillwyn Swansea" in a curve between lines appeared between 1826-1850.

Canal Age: The Duke of Bridgewater opened his famous canal in 1761, engineered by James Brindley. Its main cargo was coal that was transported on the Mersey River from Worsley to Runcorn. The Mersey and Trent Canal opened up trade for the potteries to the sea.

Carbon 14: A well-known chronometric technique used for the dating of organic material up to 70,000 years old. Based on a theory propounded by W. Libby in 1949 that cosmic rays bombard the earth's atmosphere producing neutrons, which interact with nitrogen (N14) to produce the radioactive carbon isotope (C14). The process of incorporation of the remaining C14 in a sample thus determines its age.

Cartouches: A wide blue border with three designs on a white ground occurring on one-fifth of all Gaudy Welsh tea sets.

Casting: An invention by a French chemist where sodium silicate is added to the clay mixture to decrease the drying time. The process involves pouring slip into a two-piece plaster of Paris mold which draws excess water off.

Coal: Found in abundance near the earth's surface at Staffordshire, Swansea, Sunderland, and Newcastle. It served to fire the kilns.

Coal-fired Kilns: Temperatures were difficult to control and the glaze on Gaudy Welsh was sometimes underfired. When the pores were not sealed, impurities soon gathered from the water and air, turning white into a tan or brown.

Cobalt Blue: Painted on the biscuitware as part of the Gaudy Welsh design, the blue under the glaze protects and eliminates an extra enamel firing. When applied, it is a brown hue. After firing, it often has a purplish hue resulting from manganese oxide found in British cobalt.

Common Diseases: Occupational hazards were sore eyes, scurvy, rickets, tuberculosis, other chest and lung diseases, lead poisoning, arsenic poisoning, and asthma. Some were brought on by long working hours, poor diet, clay and plaster of Paris dust, harmful smells of oils and metallic compounds, sulphur fumes, and powdered flint.

Copper Luster: Introduced about 1805 by John Hancock of England, this process dissolved about three-percent gold in nitric and hydrochloric acids which were then mixed with turpentine, linseed oil, and flowers of sulphur. Around 1840, copper luster was created from copper oxide. It lacks the brilliance of the gold luster and is often speckled.

Copyrights: Copying was prevalent among potters since design copyrights for china did not come into existence until 1839. At least a half dozen potters manufactured some form of the Oyster and Tulip patterns. Even so, only about three percent of Gaudy Welsh is marked, most coming from Wales, Sunderland, and Newcastle.

Cornish Stone: An impure feldspar or flux added to the bodies of clay to reduce their temperature as they become vitreous.

Creamware: Its color ranges from a light cream to a buff and because of a low flint content, longer drying was required and there was more spoilage. A recipe for creamware was made up of 25 parts blue clay, 22 parts black clay, 18 parts brown clay, 16 parts china clay, three parts Cornish stone and 16 parts flint.

Davies, Richard and Company: Located in Salt Meadows, South Shore, Gateshead, this firm produced printed and lusterware from 1833-1851. It is believed that they also manufactured Gaudy Welsh.

Dawson, John: Gaudy Welsh impressed "Dawson" was made between 1799 and 1836. The factory was located across from the North Hylton firm formed by the Maling family. High quality items included luster, creamware, Easter eggs, decorator tiles, and ink pots.

Day Schools: Potters' children attended these schools which were sponsored by religious groups. They began school at five years of age and continued for two or three years until they commenced working. School was held five days a week and lasted for six hours each day. Instruction included writing, spelling, reading, arithmetic, and a study of the Bible. Girls also learned how to knit and sew. Older students, supervised by the teachers, taught the young. The schools often accommodated between 150 and 400 students. Working children attended Sunday schools and evening schools held between six and eight o'clock.

Diaper Pattern: A term synonymous with the fence pattern.

Dipping Room: The location where biscuit ware was dipped into a solution containing arsenic and lead. This process exposed workers to many disabilities such as paralysis, constipation, numbness, stiffness, and bleeding. Raw lead was used in the manufacturing process since it was inexpensive. After 1901, the use of raw lead was prohibited by law, even then its use continued.

Dixon and Company: This firm of the Garrison Pottery produced and marked Gaudy Welsh between 1816-1819.

Earthenware: A typical formula for Gaudy Welsh earthenware consisted of 25 parts ball clay, 25 parts china clay, 15 parts flint. It is characterized by its opaque nature and granular consistency and was fired around 1,150 degrees Celsius.

Factory Act of 1833: A reform act instituted in 1833 which regulated the labor of children.

Family Craftsmen: A potter and the family members working in their own shop. Frequently the potter worked at other employment which was the real source of the family income.

Feldspar: A granite-like rock from Cornwall; the final ingredient in earthenware. Any of a group of crystalline minerals, aluminum silicates with either potassium, sodium, calcium, or barium in its makeup.

Fell, Thomas: A manufacturer who produced earthenware and creamware, along with Gaudy Welsh from 1830-1890, which is impressed "Fell and Co." The firm was known as St. Peter's Pottery and was established in 1817.

Flint: Heated and then ground into powder, flint creates whiteness and makes the ware less likely to shrink, crack, or warp. Used in the body and the glaze, it originated from the French coast and from Rye in southeastern England.

Flow Blue: A phenomenon where the blue ran or flowed during the biscuit firing, characteristic of Gaudy Welsh made in the 1850's. Since consumers accepted the product, it was continued. Created in the kiln during firing by adding lime or chloride of ammonia.

Flux: Used in varying amounts to create colors, it also reduced the temperature at which the glaze melted so that the fire was below the melting point of the biscuit ware.

George IV: Gaudy Welsh was manufactured about 1820, the year that George IV became King. It was said that he had a madness for building and enjoyed the decorative arts.

Glamorgan Pottery: Believed to have produced Gaudy Welsh, this firm in the Swansea area began production in 1814. Taken over by Haynes after a disagreement with Dillwyn, they copied the shapes of the Cambrian works and undercut the prices of their rival.

Green Coloration: Copper and chrome oxide were used to create this color on Gaudy Welsh.

Hawker: A peasant potter who distributed his wares from 1820-1860 by means of a pack horse. He went door-to-door, sold at local markets and fairs. Liverpool merchants exported some of the wares to the United States.

"Hungry Forties": Created by the financial crash of 1837, there was a trade and industrial depression and poor harvests escalated food prices. Slums were prevalent with people living in cellars with no sanitation or water supply. An outbreak of cholera occurred in 1848.

Imari: Gaudy Welsh forebearers from Japan on the island of Kyushu. The town in which pottery was made is called Arita, but the ware is called Imari because this is the port from which it was shipped.

"Indoor" Relief: The impoverished were sent to workhouses and the husbands and wives were separated so as not to create more children who would then become a public liability.

Jollying: A process used to create flatware and hollow ware such as cups and jugs. Plates were made by placing the clay form over a plaster or pottery mold and applying pressure. Porcelain forms were roughly created first by throwing, then the object was placed in a plaster of Paris mold to give dimension to the inside and outside shapes.

Kaolin: China clay deposited near the surface by superheated water. It is free from impurities, requires high temperatures to fuse, but lacks plasticity.

King's Rose: Decorated with a red-orange flower painted off-center with green and yellow leaves.

Lusterware: (Also Lustreware.) Produced in Scotland, Liverpool, Leeds and North and South Yorkshire by a host of potters including Mintons, Ralph Stevenson, Spode, Wedgwood, Enoch Woods and Sons, Ridgway, Copeland and Garrett, and Bailey and Batkin.

Maling, Robert: Believed to have made Gaudy Welsh, this firm was founded in Sunderland in 1762. The business was moved to the Ford Pottery in Newscastle in 1817. The impressed "Maling" mark has been discovered on several patterns.

Master Craftsmen: Each master hired apprentices who were first trained and then later worked for pay after learning their trade.

Meir, John: An early producer of Gaudy Welsh who commenced business at Tunstall in 1812. Earthenware was fabricated at the Greengates Pottery. In 1837, the firm's name was changed from "John Meir" to "John Meir and Son." They produced earthenware until 1897.

Mellor, Venable and Company: Located in Burslem, this company sent handpainted earthenware to the United States. It is possible that they made Gaudy Welsh.

Merchant Employers: In this arrangement, a merchant hired potters to make wares which he then sold. The process was probably in vogue after 1830.

Mould Running: Performed by children, from four to six hundred trips were required be made to the ovens where the moulds dried. Extreme changes in temperature created bronchial and rheumatic symptoms for the youths.

"Old Poor Law": Established during Elizabethan time, each parish established taxes so that the poor could be cared for when large groups of workers had no employment. This law encouraged employers to pay insufficient wages and created higher taxes in the parish. The Poor Law was amended in 1834 and parishes were made into unions to spread the costs evenly.

"Outdoor" Relief: Poor persons received assistance while living at home.

Pattern Names: Gaudy Welsh has been called Welsh Luster, Cottage Ware, Peasant Enamel, and Cottage Swansea and possibly three hundred patterns with variations exist manufactured by numerous potters.

Pearlware: Small amounts of cobalt added to the cream glaze to give it additional whiteness, called "pearl ware" by Wedgwood.

Plastic Clays: Clays which are whiter and have fewer impurities originating in Dorset and Devon.

Potteries: A collective term for the Stoke-on-Trent area in Staffordshire where numerous firms were located that produced the greatest amount of Gaudy Welsh.

Potworks: From 1710 to 1800, this number increased from 47 to 124. As factories grew, more people were employed. By 1833, Wood had 1,100 workers, Minton and Copeland, 700 each; Meigh and Hicks, 600; Ridgeway, 500 and Alcock, 400.

Prattware: Made by Felix Pratt between 1790 and 1830, these relief molded, rustic jugs were brightly colored. The white or cream colored earthenware was in shades of yellow, orange, blue, black, and purple. Other potters such as Gordons, Prestonpans, Barker and Hawley, and Enoch Wood copied Prattware.

Pressing: To roll clay to a desired thickness and then press it into a mold. Handles for Gaudy Welsh forms were made in this fashion and attached with slip.

Pug Mill: A machine that came into vogue around 1860, the device had a group of blades which rotated, kneading the clay and mixing the airless batch so that it could be formed into objects.

Queen's Rose: Closely resembles King's Rose but the flower is pink and the other designs are more delicate.

Railway: In the late 1840's over 7,000 miles of track were completed in Britain's rail system. The owners bought out the canals, some were closed, others raised the charges so that canals could no longer compete.

Recreations: Saturday night and Sunday were the times for leisure activities after a long work week. Card playing, drinking, cribbage, billiards, and jigs, polkas, and country dancing were popular pastimes.

Red and Burnt Orange Colors: Iron oxide was used to achieve these hues on Gaudy Welsh.

Repeal of Combination Acts: Laws which did not allow workers to strike, seek better wages, or better working conditions.

Reproductions: Gaudy Welsh was copied during this century by many Staffordshire potteries including Charles Allerton and Sons, Edward Walley, James Kent, Old Castle, and Lingard.

Sansai: A later Imari decoration having alternate panels of blue and white with flowers and other figures in red and blue, highlighted with gold.

Scourer: A worker whose responsibility was to smooth biscuit objects by scouring with sandpaper and stone.

Scouring Room: The location where objects were sent to remove any roughness. Workers coughed a great deal here because of the profusion of dust in the air.

Sedimentary Clay: An impure ball clay having animal matter, minerals, or plants in its consistency. Found at the sites of former rivers, in lake beds, and dried estuaries. Prized for its low firing temperature and its plasticity.

Shanghai: Another name for the Dogwood pattern.

Sheriff Hill Pottery: Manufactured Gaudy Welsh. The firm was owned by the Patterson family from 1827-1892. The factory was in Gateshead just across the Tyne from Newcastle.

"Slop" Bowl: A repository for used tea leaves and other table scraps.

South Wales Pottery: This firm produced earthenware, porcelain, and transfer and handpainted wares. Located at Llanelly, near Swansea, the factory began in 1840 under the guidance of William Chambers, Junior. Gaudy Welsh made by the firm is impressed "South Wales Pottery."

Spatterware: A colorful ware with applied sponge decorations in green, blue, pink, brown, yellow, and purple borders. The central designs may feature tulips, beehives, schoolhouses, peafowl, and other figures. Made in soft paste, ironstone, creamware, and pearlware. It dates between 1790 and 1840.

Spode: A manufacturer that may have produced Gaudy Welsh, they impressed their wares "S" which has been found on the Oyster pattern.

Staffordshire: A center for British pottery, the majority of Gaudy Welsh was produced there. In 1710, some 500 individuals were employed in the industry, this number increased to 15,000 by 1785. By the end of the Gaudy Welsh period in 1860, the workers numbered close to 28,000.

Steel Ships: Ocean going ships were placed in production by 1850, an outstanding vessel was called the *Great Eastern* built in 1858, it averaged 14 knots on its first Atlantic crossing. By 1830, British ships were wooden hulled, navigated by wind and sail. Some 500,000 pounds of pottery were exported in one year, half went to the United States, some was shipped to Holland and Germany.

Stone China: A formula for this ware consisted of 10 parts blue clay, 33 parts china clay, 50 parts Cornish stone, and seven parts flint.

Sunderland: This ware possesses a marbled or spotted decoration which shades from pink to purple. A gold compound was applied over the white body to develop many shades of luster, the shade being determined by the metallic film's thickness. Manufactured by many firms including Adams, Bailey and Batkin, Copeland and Garrett, Wedgwood, and Enoch Wood.

Synonyms: Gaudy Welsh has also been called Welsh Luster, Peasant Enamel, Cottage Ware, and Cottage Swansea.

Throwing: Clay is placed on the potter's wheel and centered. With the turning of the wheel, the potter's skill gives the object its appropriate shape. To build the vessel's sides, the potter presses in the middle and supports the sides with his other hand. Walls may be made thinner and taller by exerting pressure between the fingers on one side and utilizing the thumb on the other. Concave or convex shapes may be created by exerting pressure between the fingers on one hand and using the palm of the other.

Turnpike Trusts: Groups maintained the roads and charged tolls to create revenues. The trusts rose from 150 to 1,100 during 1750-1830; this accounted for about one-fifth of the road throughout the country.

Ultraviolet Lamp: The black light is invaluable in determining repairs on painting, glass, china, porcelain, paper, ivory, scrimshaw, textiles, and numerous other materials. With china and porcelain, the light will show up glued areas, mends, and touch-up painted areas. Small battery operated devices are available which may be carried easily and used at shows, flea markets, etc.

Wages: Adult workers were paid by the piece. Men earned 25 to 28 shillings per week, women got 8 to 9 shillings, and children received 2 shillings and 6 pence paid from the adult wages.

Walker, Thomas: Located in Tunstall, this firm operated from 1845 to 1851, they are known to have sent handpainted wares to the United States.

Walley, Edward: Located at Villa Pottery in Cobridge, he began his operation with Elijah Jones in 1841. By 1845, he worked alone making earthenware, ironstone, and parian until 1865. He is most noted for his decoration of Gaudy Welsh on ironstone. Some examples are impressed "PARIS WHITE IRONSTONE CHINA" around the edge of a circle, with the word "WALLEY" placed in the middle of a circle.

Wedging: Kneading and cutting plastic clay, throwing one piece upon another in order to obtain a uniform texture free from air pockets. Much clay used in the manufacturer of Gaudy Welsh was prepared in this manner.

Yellow Color: Iron, chrome, and antimony were used to create this oxide.

A potter's wheel, circa 1843, left to right, wheel turner, ball maker, and thrower.
Illustration from *The Penny Magazine*, February, 1843.

GAUDY WELSH
DESCRIPTIONS AND PRICES

Footed compote, Urn II, diameter 9½"; 4¾" high, marked "X - 710" in red on the base. $290.00.

Scalloped and footed compote, 10" diameter; 5½" high. $260.00.

Compote, lavishly decorated inside and out. 11¾" diameter; 6¾" high. $250.00. (A comparison piece, Mason's Amherst/Japan, not Gaudy Welsh.)

Vine I handled sugar bowl, gallery top, pointed finial, bell-shaped lid, octagonal body. 9" high. $150.00.

Pair of Tulip pattern covered sugar bowls. Ornate applied handles, ring finials. Left - 6¾" high. $125.00. Right - footed, 7" high. $145.00.

Squatty sugar bowl, applied handles, pointed finial, overhanging lid, 6½" high, Carousel pattern. $150.00.

Sugar bowl with large fancy handles, ring finial, six-footed base, 7" high. Basket of Flowers pattern. $145.00.

Left Photo: Sugar bowl with U-shaped handles, overhanging lid, button finial, four-footed base, 7" high, Castle pattern. $155.00.

Right Photo: Sugar bowl with thorn handles, inset lid, ring finial, six-sided raised base, 7" high. Columbine pattern. $160.00.

Two footed creamers, Tulip variants. Both have six raised appendages, applied handles. Tallest example is 6¾" high. Left - $100.00, right - $110.00.

Three varied shaped creamers. Center and right examples are footed; tallest piece is 5¾" high. Columbine variants. Left - $85.00, center - $90.00, right - $95.00.

Three assorted creamers in the Oyster pattern. Note the varying artistic application. Tallest example is 4¾" high. Left - $75.00, center - $110.00, right - $95.00.

Creamer, graceful sleigh top, 5" high, Powys pattern. $120.00.

Grape design ornate handled creamer. Raised embossed design in the mold. 7½" high. $185.00.

Rare creamer, ridged handle, 4¾" high. Village pattern. $225.00.

Miniature grouping showing two baptismal mugs plus a cup and saucer. Left: Tiny Grape mug - $125.00. Center: Grape cup and saucer - $75.00. Right: Tulip mug - $100.00.

Left to right: Rare Tulip egg cup - $110.00; Oyster mug - $65.00; very rare miniature pitcher and bowl set, 3½" high, Tulip pattern - $210.00.

Two miniature examples. Left: bowl, 4½" diameter, Grape pattern - $75.00. Right: Grape mug - $65.00.

Upper Left Photo: Very rare Chinoisserie pitcher in mint condition, obverse, 5¼" high. Upper Right Photo: Reverse side of pitcher. Lower Left Photo: Frontal view of the pitcher. Note unusual masked and bearded spout. $250.00.

Miniature grouping showing two creamers and a bowl, Chinoisserie transfer design. Creamers - $75.00 each; Bowl - $65.00.

A grouping of two miniature mugs with a rare potty in the center. Only one panel shows the Chinoisserie decoration. Left and right: $60.00-65.00; center - $100.00.

Two creamers, tallest example 4¼" high. Left: Cherry Tree pattern - $95.00. Right: Asian pattern - $85.00.

Rare urn, Pot de Fleurs II pattern. $300.00.

Left Photo: Very rare miniature Oyster creamer with figural head on spout (frontal view), 2¼" high. $225.00.

Right Photo: Side view of the creamer.

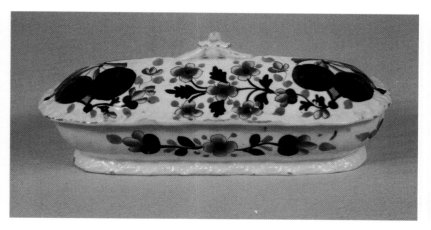

Very rare handled loving cup in Rainbow pattern, 3⅛" high. $225.00.

Extremely rare covered rectangular quill holder, unusual finial. 8" long; 3¼" high. $325.00.

Two waste bowls, Tulip variants. Left example is decorated both inside and outside, 6¼" diameter. $75.00. Right example is 6" diameter. $65.00.

Three waste bowls. Left: Fruit - $85.00, center: Oyster - $65.00, right: Feather - $85.00.

Very ornate teapot with footed base, 7" high, numbered "807" in green on the base, Venus pattern. $210.00.

Another squatty teapot, Tulip design, well decorated, fancy handle and spout, 5½" high. $200.00.

Teapot with ear-shaped handle that is not attached at the top, button finial, 7" high, Powys pattern. $250.00.

Eight inch teapot, bell-shaped lid, ring finial, four inset panels of flowers, six-footed base. $150.00.

Teapot having a fancy handle, much pink and gold luster, 7" high, Carousel pattern. $185.00.

Three colorful and unusual shaped milk pitchers. Left: Grape - $125.00. Center: Rare, flat medallion-shaped sides, much green and gold has been used in decorating - $285.00. Right: Raised portions are decorated, Flower Basket on its side. $145.00.

A pair of cups and saucers. Left: Early and without a handle, much blue and luster, Pinwheel pattern. $95.00. Right: Tulip - $75.00.

Left: Lustered cup and saucer with a profusion of blue. $65.00. Right: Grape patterned cup and saucer. $75.00.

Two cups and saucers with cartouches. Both cups are decorated on the inside. Left: Fruit pattern - $75.00. Right: Columbine pattern - $70.00.

Unusual handled cups and saucers. Left: Scallop - $65.00. Right: Tulip - $65.00.

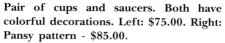

Pair of cups and saucers. Both have colorful decorations. Left: $75.00. Right: Pansy pattern - $85.00.

Left: Geranium cup and saucer - $100.00. Right: Drape pattern cup and saucer - $95.00. Note the handle styles.

Both cups are decorated on the inside. Left: Village cup and saucer. $175.00. Right: Flower Basket II cup and saucer. $85.00.

A pair of cups and saucers with colorful and well-proportioned decor. Left: Sunflower - $75.00. Right: Floret - $80.00.

A portion of a child's tea set including a cup and saucer and a plate in the Wagon Wheel pattern. The plate is numbered "16" in red on the base. Plate - $85.00. Cup and saucer - $95.00.

Additional pieces from a child's tea set including a covered teapot, covered sugar and creamer, all are numbered "16" in red on the bottom. The complete set is in mint condition and consists of six place settings in the Wagon Wheel pattern. A rare find. $1,500.00 for the set.

Two plates with cartouches, Left: Feather - $85.00. Right: Columbine - $90.00.

Two unusually shaped plates. Left: Pinwheel - $85.00. Right: Carousel - $95.00.

Two plates with cartouches done with transfers. Left example is quite unusual with its orange decoration, gold scrolls. Two panels depict a mother and child, one panel with a man and a woman with a parasol, and the fourth panel shows a boy with sheep. $85.00. Right plate has orange decor, gold scrolls, three panels with fruit and flowers. In the center is a bird on a branch. Nightingale pattern - $75.00.

Left: A profusion of blue with minimal orange and green coloration. $75.00. Right: Pinwheel with Flowers - $125.00.

Left: Vine plate - $70.00. Right: Delicate floral border and interior. $70.00.

Left: Plate in Pansy pattern - $90.00. Right: Nebula pattern - $80.00.

Two very decorative plates. Left: Urn with Flowers - $90.00. Right: Tricorn - $75.00.

The left example is a plate in Flower Basket II pattern. $85.00. On the right is a biscuit tray (a scarce and unusual shape) in the Tulip pattern. $95.00.

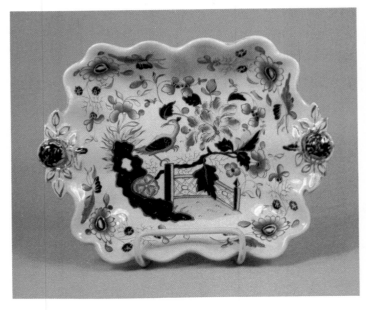

A nice deeply scalloped edge dish with a colorful bird design, numbered "107" on the bottom in red. Peacock pattern - $85.00.

Cambrian Rose pitcher, red number "8" on the seven-sided base. Ornate handle, ruffled top, 6¾" to the top of the handle. $225.00.

Mint condition Nebula teapot. Serpent spout, fancy scrolled handle, inset lid with large rosette finial. Top of the body form appears like an inverted plate. Excellent artistic rendering and shading of flowers. $300.00.

Pair of cups and saucers. Left: Oyster pattern - $80.00. Right: Pink and russet flowers with green leaves between cobalt scallops. $75.00.

Left: Grape cup and saucer - $95.00. Right: Rare Grape cup and saucer. The back of the saucer is impressed with the "WOOD" logo. $125.00.

Left: "Bleeding Heart and Fern" cup and saucer - $75.00. Right: Urn II cup and saucer - $95.00.

Two mint condition Butterfly scalloped plates. Left: 9" diameter - $110.00. Right: 10" diameter - $125.00. Both impressed on the back with an eagle facing to the left, having his wings spread and holding a branch in his left talon and arrows in his right talon.

Left: Obverse of "Pagoda" milk pitcher. Ornate handle, scalloped top and base, colorfully decorated. Right: Reverse side of pitcher. $185.00.

Cup and saucer with floral transfer on the cup's exterior with two interior views showing a young man picking flowers for his girlfriend and a young man bundling sticks. The saucer panels reveal the same two views plus a young girl flying a kite. $75.00.

Above: Very rare and well-decorated snake handled jug in Sunflower pattern. 5¾" high, octagonal base and spout, scalloped top. Right: Close-up view of the jug with emphasis upon the decoration and the snake handle. $285.00.

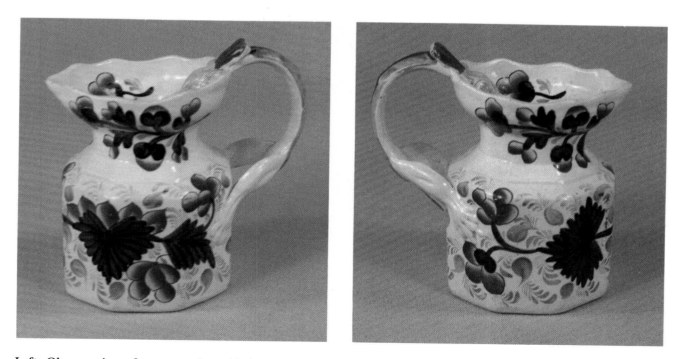

Left: Obverse view of very rare jug with legendary stylized dragon handle. Octagonal with nine-sided ruffled spout, 4" high, Grape pattern. $235.00. Right: Reverse view of jug.

The dragon's head with its tongue sticking out is shown on the interior of the same jug.

A view of the back of the jug exhibiting the dragon's body and back legs.

Set of six cups and saucers, slight scalloped edges, Vine pattern. Saucers, 5¾" in diameter; cups, 2" high. Set -$390.00.

Plate with beautifully executed Grape design, 7¼" diameter, $125.00.

Very rare handled mug with verse and decoration. Ear handle with thumb accessory, 4" high; 4¼" diameter. $425.00.

Close-up of mug showing the calligraphy done in russet which reads:

What heals wives broken hearts

And dries the falling tear

What gives their children bread

And gives them clothes to wear

Teetotalism

The American Temperance Union in 1836 decided that abstinence from hard liquor was not enough. The New Pledge that it introduced required signers to abstain from hard liquor as well as wine, beer, and hard cider. One who abstained from all alcoholic beverages was called a teetotaler, with emphasis on the initial "t" of total (T-total - complete total abstinence or total with a capital "T.") Teetotally (T-totally) was first used by Parson Mason Locke Weems in America in 1807. Teetotal meaning total abstinence from all alcoholic drink was first used by Richard Turner, Preston, England, in 1833.

Left: Cup and saucer, Elfin Cap pattern. Saucer's diameter is 5¾"; cup is 2¼" high. Right: Cup and saucer in the Peppermint design. Saucer is 5¾" in diameter; cup is 2⅛" high. Value of each set - $80.00.

Pronounced scalloped edges appear on both sets of cups and saucers. Left: Burma decor. Saucer is 5¾" in diameter; cup is 2" high. $80.00. Right: Violet design. Saucer has a diameter of 5⅝"; cup is 2" high. $65.00.

Very rare signed cup and saucer in the Grape pattern. Scalloped edges, both impressed "WEDGWOOD" on the reverse. Diameter of saucer is 5¼"; cup is 2⅛" high. $150.00.

PRICE GUIDE

Bowl, 10½" diameter, Flower Basket $200.00
Bowl, 6¼", Oyster $60.00
Bowl, 8" diameter, Oyster $150.00
Bowl, 7½" diameter, Wagon Wheel $75.00
Cake Plate, Feather $60.00
Compote, 10¼" diameter, 5¾" high,
    Morning Glory $285.00
Condiment Set, Tulip $105.00
Creamer, Daisy and Chain $80.00
Creamer, Flower Basket $110.00
Creamer, 4", Grape $50.00
Creamer, large, Grape $75.00
Creamer, Mask Spout, 2½" high $75.00
Creamer, Morning Glory $100.00
Creamer, 3½" high, Oyster $90.00
Creamer, large, Oyster $125.00
Creamer, Shanghai $150.00
Creamer, Strawberry $110.00
Creamer, 5¼" high, Tulip $110.00
Cup and Saucer, Carnation $90.00
Cup and Saucer, Columbine $95.00
Cup and Saucer, set of 6, Feather design $300.00
Cup and Saucer, Feather $50.00
Cup and Saucer, Flower Basket $85.00
Cup and Saucer, handleless, Grape $90.00
Cup and Saucer, Grape and Lily $90.00
Cup and Saucer, Morning Glory $95.00
Cup and Saucer, Oyster $80.00
Cup and Saucer, Pennant $95.00
Cup and Saucer, Poppy $75.00
Cup and Saucer, set of 6, Rhoda design $250.00
Cup and Saucer, Seeing Eye $125.00
Cup and Saucer, Tulip $90.00
Cup and Saucer, Wagon Wheel $85.00
Cup and Saucer, Wildflowers, cobalt blue $60.00
Dish, cheese, Morning Glory $135.00
Dinner Service, 56 pieces, Flower Basket
(16 dinner plates, 28 luncheon plates,
8 ovoid salad plates, 4 graduated platters) $1,800.00
Dish, serving, 9", Tulip $50.00
Jug, 4½", Oyster $85.00
Mug, handled, Flower Basket $150.00
Mug, 3" high, Oyster $145.00
Mug, 4⅛", Strawberry $150.00
Mug, Tulip $85.00
Mug, 2¾", Wagon Wheel $90.00
Pitcher, 4¾" high, Glamorgan $75.00
Pitcher, 6½" high, Allerton, circa 1890,
    Morning Glory $90.00
Pitcher, 3½" x 3¼", Oyster $90.00
Pitcher, 4½" x 4½", Oyster $100.00
Pitcher, 5½", Oyster $120.00
Pitcher, milk, Oyster $160.00
Pitcher, 5⅝", Pagoda $100.00
Pitcher, 5" high, snake handle, Sunflower $200.00

Pitcher, milk, Tulip $200.00
Pitcher, 8½", milk, Wagon Wheel $225.00
Plate, 5½", Columbine $65.00
Plate, 8¼", Columbine $95.00
Plate, Daisy and Chain $125.00
Plate, 8", Feather $65.00
Plate, 8½" square, Flower Basket $150.00
Plate, 12 sided, purple luster trim,
    8⅞", Flower Basket $85.00
Plate, 9", Flower Basket $150.00
Plate, 9½", Flower Basket $165.00
Plate, 8½" square, Grape $110.00
Plate, 8", Morning Glory $85.00
Plate, 9", Morning Glory $110.00
Plate, 10", Morning Glory $135.00
Plate, 6", dessert, Oyster $60.00
Plate, 8¾", Oyster $125.00
Plate, 9½", Oyster $140.00
Plate, 5½", Shanghai $110.00
Plate, 8¼", Strawberry $150.00
Plate, 6" diameter, Tulip $60.00
Plate, 7¾", Tulip $75.00
Plate, 9", Tulip $90.00
Plate, 7½", Urn $125.00
Plate, 5½", Wagon Wheel $75.00
Plate, 7½", Wagon Wheel $90.00
Plate, 8¾", Wagon Wheel $110.00
Platter, 14½", Morning Glory $165.00
Platter, Wagon Wheel $140.00
Soup Plate, 10" diameter,
    pink border, flange rim $100.00
Spill Holders, 4⅜" high, pair, Strawberry $300.00
Sugar, covered, Daisy and Chain $150.00
Sugar, covered, Flower Basket $105.00
Sugar Bowl, luster, lion's head handles,
    lidded, Flower Basket $155.00
Sugar/Creamer, covered sugar, Grape and Lily $265.00
Sugar, 6¾" high, covered, Tulip $150.00
Teapot, covered, Cornflower $175.00
Teapot, covered, Daisy and Chain $200.00
Teapot, covered, 5½", Morning Glory $225.00
Teapot, covered, Strawberry $210.00
Teapot, covered, Tulip $200.00
Teapot, 7¼", ornate cover, Tulip $235.00
Teapot, Wagon Wheel $200.00
Tea Set, 17 pieces, Columbine $775.00
Tea Set, Morning Glory
15 pieces, creamer, sugar bowl, 6 cups and saucers $900.00
Tea Set, child's, 3 pieces, Oyster $225.00
Tea Set, 11 pieces, 4 cups and saucers, Tulip $600.00
Tea Set, child's grouping, Flow Blue,
    Wagon Wheel $575.00
Tureen, 9½" wide, footed, Urn $275.00
Vegetable Bowl, round, Morning Glory $90.00
Waste Bowl, 6⅜" diameter, Tulip $110.00

TERMS USED BY POTTERS

Bags: Chimneys or fire brick walls constructed to protect the ware from the flame.

Baiting: The feeding of fuel during the firing.

Bat: A flat slab of biscuit, plaster, or fire clay.

Biscuit: Fired but unglazed clay.

Blowing: A shattered clay shape occurring when biscuiting, usually due to hurried firing or sudden heat.

Blunger: A machine used to mix clay.

Bungs: Piles of filled saggars.

Chuck or Chum: A cone or cap used to support shapes while they are being turned on a lathe.

Clamming: Wet sand, siftings, or marl applied to cracks in the doors of the kilns so that heat is retained during the firing.

Craze: Minute cracks that appear in a poorly fitting glaze.

Drawing: Unpacking the kiln after it has been fired.

Engobe: An outer covering of slip usually applied to inferior examples to improve their appearance.

Fat: Clays that are characterized as being greasy or sticky.

Fettle: A touching-up process used to remove casting lines, traces of seams, etc.

Glost: The glazed ware, a term applied to the glaze in firing, as glost-oven.

Green: Clay shapes before biscuiting.

Jigger: A wheel on which shapes are molded with the aid of a profile or a jolley.

Joggle: The key in a mold used to insure a correct adjustment and prevent slipping.

Lawn: A fine mesh gauze through which glazes are strained.

Long: Clay is termed "long" when it is very tenacious and ductile.

Muffle: The fire-clay box or interior of a small kiln. Also applied to any kiln to which flames have no access to the inside.

Natch: See Joggle.

Oxidizing: Ordinary firing methods give an atmosphere where there is sufficient oxygen to consume combustible gases and carbon. When an excess of oxygen is present, it causes a reaction known as oxidizing.

Pitchers: Finely ground biscuit added to some clays to increase their porosity and refractories. Molds made of such clays and fired are termed "pitcher molds."

Potsherds: A broken pot or biscuit, also used for pitchers.

Potting: A colloquialism used to describe the ceramic industry.

Pugging: A roll of infusible clay placed between each saggar when building bungs.

Reducing: The reaction that accompanies the introduction of gas or smoke containing carbon in a very finely divided state into a kiln during the process of glaze firing. Reduction is used widely to obtain fine luster effects.

Refractory: That which is infusible and hard.

Rich: A term describing long and fusible clay, such as red clay.

Riffle: A steel grooved and toothed plaster tool.

Saggars: Also called seggers. These are the fire receptacles where the glazed ware is set during firing.

Setters: Supports used when packing friable biscuit.

Short: A clay that crumbles or is difficult to pull up on the wheel.

Sieve: Also called a lawn. More correctly, a screen used with slip or clay.

Slip: Sieved clay or paste that is a creamy liquid used for casting, engobes, and slip decorating.

Slub or Slurry: Clay that is mixed with water but not sieved, as with slip.

Spy: A small hole, kept sealed, through which cones and tests are observed.

Stunt: Also termed dunt, meaning to crack or split when cooling.

Turning: Shaving down of a clay shape on a lathe, to create a lightness and proper finish.

U.G.: Underglaze abbreviation, applied to colors.

Vent: A hole which aids in the even distribution of fire in the kiln. Also it accelerates in cooling off.

Waster: A spoiled or defective pot, termed "seconds."

Wedging: A beating or slamming operation employed to expel air just before the clay is used by the thrower.

Whirler: A circular support which pivots on its center and is used in casting or banding.

Illustrations from *The Penny Magazine,* February 1843.

Top Left: Grinding clay and flint.

Bottom Left: Placing fabricated objects into seggars.

Above: Placing the seggars into the biscuit kiln.

Illustrations from *Pottery* by George J. Cox

An Egyptian potter, 2000 B.C.

An early Greek kiln.

An Indian potter, 2000 B.C.

A potter in the 1500's forming a vessel using a table top kick wheel.

Illustrations from *Pottery* by George J. Cox

A typical wooden kick wheel used for throwing objects.

A potter at work hollowing the ball.

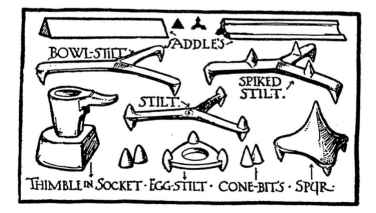

Stilts and spurs are used in a glaze kiln instead of saddles to prevent the objects from sticking to the floors and shelves.

BIBLIOGRAPHY

Alridge, Eileen. *Porcelain.* New York: Bantam Books, 1971.

Banning, E.B. "Revolution in Radiocarbon Dating," *Antiquity,* November 1979, pages 226-228.

Barton, R.M. *History of the Cornish China Clay Industry.* D. Bradford Barton, Ltd., Cornwall, 1966.

Boger, L.A. *The Dictionary of World Pottery and Porcelain.* New York: Charles Scribner's Sons, 1971.

Brears, Peter. *The English Country Pottery.* David and Charles, Newton Abbot, 1971.

Chappell, J. *The Potter's Complete Book of Clay and Glazes.* New York: Watson-Guptill Publications, 1977, pages 18-24.

Charles, B.H. *Pottery and Porcelain.* London: David and Charles, 1974, pages 277-279.

Children's Employment Commission, *Second Report of the Commissioners,* 1842.

Comstock, Helen (ed.) *The Concise Encyclopedia of American Antiques.* New York: Hawthorn Books, Incorporated, 1969.

Cottrell, L. (ed.) *The Concise Encyclopedia of Archaeology.* New York: Hawthorn, 1971.

Cox, George J. *Pottery, For Artists, Craftmen, and Teachers.* New York: The Macmillan Company, 1914.

Coysh, A.W. *Blue-Printed Earthenware 1800-1850.* David and Charles, Newton Abbot, 1972.

Evans, William. "Art and History of the Potting Business, 1846," *Journal of Ceramic History,* No. 3, 1970.

Factories Inquiry Commission of Employment of Children, *Minutes of Evidence,* 1833.

Fournier, R. *Illustrated Dictionary of Practical Pottery.* New York: Van Nostrand Reinhold, 1977.

Gay, P.W. & Smyth, R.L. *The British Pottery Industry.* Butterworths, London, 1974.

Godden, Geoffrey, A. *Encyclopedia of British Pottery and Porcelain Marks.* Bonanza Books, New York, 1964.

Green, D. *Understanding Pottery Glazes.* London: Faber and Faber, Ltd., 1963.

Grisson, Betty. "Edward Walley's Gaudy Ironstone." *The Spinning Wheel's Complete Book of Antiques.* Grosset & Dunlap, New York, 1972.

Hadfield, Charles. *British Canals.* Phoenix House, London. 1959.

Haggar, Reginald. *English Country Pottery.* Phoenix House, London, 1950.

Hamer, F. *The Potter's Dictionary of Materials and Techniques.* London: Pitman Publishing, 1975, pages 205-206.

Harbottle, G. and others. "C-14 Dating of Small Samples by Proportional Counting," *Science,* November 1979, pages 683-685.

Hillier, Bevis. *Pottery and Porcelain 1700-1914.* Weidenfeld and Nicholson, London, 1968.

Hughes, Bernard. *The Collector's Pocket Book of China.* Award Books, New York, 1970.

Hughes, Bernard. *Victorian Pottery and Porcelain.* Spring Books, London, 1969.

Hughes, G. Bernard. *English and Scottish Earthenware.* Abbey Fine Arts, London.

Hughes, Peter. *Welsh China.* National Museum of Wales, Cardiff, 1972.

Ketchum, William C., Jr. *Pottery and Porcelain Collectors Handbook.* New York: Funk and Wagnalls Company, 1971.

Kovel, Ralph and Terry. *Know Your Antiques.* New York: Crown Publishers, Incorporated, 1967.

Mankowitz, Wolf and Reginald Haggar. *The Concise Encyclopedia of English Pottery and Porcelain.* Hawthorne Books, New York.

McClinton, Katharine Morrison. *A Handbook of Popular Antiques.* New York: Bonanza Books, 1946.

Moore, N. Hudson. *The Old China Book.* New York: Tudor Publishing Company, 1946.

Nelson, G.C. *Ceramics,* fourth edition. New York: Holt, Rinehart and Winston, 1978.

Ormsbee, Thomas H. *English China and Its Marks.* New York: Deerfield Editions, Limited, 1959.

Owen, Harold. *The Staffordshire Potter.* Grant Richards, London, 1901.

Rackham, Bernard & H. Read. *English Pottery.* E.P. Publishing Ltd., London, 1972.

Rado, Paul. *An Introduction to the Technology of Pottery.* Oxford: Pergamon Press, Ltd., 1969, pages 148-152.

Rhodes, D. *Clay and Glazes for the Potter.* New York: Pitman Publishing Corporation, 1957.

Robacker, Earl F. *Touch of the Dutchland.* New York: A.S. Barnes and Company, Incorporated, 1965.

Rolt, L.T.C. *The Potters Field: History of the South Devon Ball Clay Industry.* David & Charles, 1974.

Russel, A. *From Clay to Art.* Philadelphia: Dorrance and Company, Inc., 1978.

Sanders, H.H. *Glazes for Special Effects.* New York: Watson-Guptill, 1974.

Sapiro, M. *Clay, The Potter's Wheel.* Worcester, Mass.: Davis Publications, 1977, p. 14 –.

Schaun, George and Virginia. *Everyday Life In Colonial Pennsylvania.* Annapolis, Maryland: Greenberry Publications, 1963.

Shafer, T. "Overglaze Enamels, Low-Temperature Glazes and Lusters," Ceramics Monthly, September 1976, pages 44-49.

Shafer, T. *Pottery Decoration.* New York: Watson-Guptill Publications, 1976.

Shaw, Kenneth. *Ceramic Colours and Pottery Decoration,* revised edition. London: Maclaren and Sons, Ltd., 1968, pages 155-160.

Shaw, Simeon. *History of the Staffordshire Potteries.* Charles, London, 1829.

Shedd, Nelita Salmon. "Some Clarifying Facts About Gaudy Welsh," *Antiques Journal,* January 1966.

Shenker, Israel. "From the villages of Stoke-on-Trent, a river of china," *Smithsonian,* March 1989, pages 130-134, continued 136 and 138-139.

Soderland, Jean R. (ed.) *William Penn and the founding of Pennsylvania, 1680-1684,* University of Pennsylvania Press, 1983.

Southwell, S. *Painting China and Porcelain.* New York: Sterling Publishing Company, 1983.

Stamp, L. Dudley & Beaver, Stanley H. *The British Isles.* London: Longmans, Green and Company, 1941.

Thomas, John. *The Rise of the Staffordshire Potteries.* Adams & Dart, Bath, 1971.

Torbet, L. (ed.) *The Encyclopedia of Crafts,* volume 1. New York: Charles Scribner's Sons, 1980, pages 174-176.

Trimble, Alberta C. *Modern Porcelain.* New York: Bonanza, 1962.

Turner, William. *Ceramics of Swansea and Nantgarw.* London, 1897.

Weatherill, Lorna. *The Pottery Trade and North Staffordshire.* 1660-1760, Manchester University Press, 1971.

Williams, Howard Y. *Gaudy Welsh China.* Des Moines, Iowa: Wallace-Homestead Book Company, 1978.

Woody, E.S. *Pottery on the Wheel.* New York: Farrar, Straus and Giroux, 1975.

Zelinsky, Wilbur. *The Cultural Geography of the United States.* Englewood Cliffs, New Jersey: Prentice-Hall, 1973.

Schroeder's Antiques Price Guide

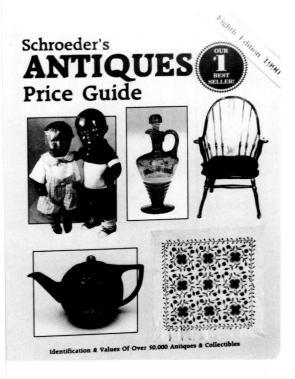

Schroeder's Antiques Price Guide has become THE household name in the antiques & collectibles industry. Our team of editors work year around with more than 200 contributors to bring you our #1 best-selling book on antiques & collectibles.

With more than 50,000 items identified & priced, Schroeder's is a must for the collector & dealer alike. If it merits the interest of today's collector, you'll find it in Schroeder's. Each subject is represented with histories and background information. In addition, hundreds of sharp original photos are used each year to illustrate not only the rare and unusual, but the everyday "fun-type" collectibles as well -- not postage stamp pictures, but large close-up shots that show important details clearly.

Our editors compile a new book each year. Never do we merely change prices. Accuracy is our primary aim. Prices are gathered over the entire year previous to publication, from ads and personal contacts. Then each category is thoroughly checked to spot inconsistencies, listings that may not be entirely reflective of actual market dealings, and lines too vague to be of merit. Only the best of the lot remains for publication. You'll find Schroeder's Antiques Price Guide the one to buy for factual information and quality.

No dealer, collector or investor can afford not to own this book. It is available from your favorite bookseller or antiques dealer at the low price of $12.95. If you are unable to find this price guide in your area, it's available from Collector Books, P.O. Box 3009, Paducah, KY 42001 at $12.95 plus $2.00 for postage and handling.

8½ x 11", 608 Pages   **$12.95**

COLLECTOR BOOKS
A Division of Schroeder Publishing Co., Inc.